THE REDISCOVERY OF MAN

THE MACMILLAN COMPANY
NEW YORK · BOSTON · CHICAGO · DALLAS
ATLANTA · SAN FRANCISCO

MACMILLAN AND CO., LIMITED
LONDON · BOMBAY · CALCUTTA · MADRAS
MELBOURNE

THE MACMILLAN COMPANY
OF CANADA, LIMITED
TORONTO

THE
REDISCOVERY
OF MAN

By

Henry C. Link, Ph.D.

NEW YORK

THE MACMILLAN COMPANY

1939

*Set up and electrotyped. Published October, 1938.
Reprinted October, 1938 (twice); November, 1938;
February, 1939.*

PRINTED IN THE UNITED STATES OF AMERICA
AMERICAN BOOK—STRATFORD PRESS, INC., NEW YORK

Dedicated to the Memory of
THOMAS CARLYLE
especially his great chapter
The Everlasting No

Thus has the bewildered Wanderer to stand, as so many have done, shouting question after question into the Sibyl-cave of Destiny, and receive no answer but an Echo. It is all a grim Desert, this once-fair world of his; wherein is heard only the howling of wild beasts, or the shrieks of despairing, hate-filled men, and no Pillar of Cloud by day, and no Pillar of Fire by night, any longer guides the Pilgrim. To such length has the spirit of Inquiry carried him. . . .

*   *   *   *   *   *   *

Thus has the *Everlasting No* pealed authoritatively through all the recesses of my Being, of my Me. . . . The Everlasting No had said: "Behold thou art father-less, outcast, and the Universe is mine (the Devil's)"; to which my whole Me now made answer: "I am not thine, but Free, and forever hate thee!"

It is from this hour that I incline to date my Spiritual New-birth, or Baphometic Fire-baptism; perhaps I directly thereupon began to be a Man.

—THOMAS CARLYLE

A LETTER TO A PESSIMISTIC FRIEND

By the Author

July 7, 1938

DEAR FRANK,

Now that you have put your pessimism into practice, and retired to your farm, I hope that you will soon feel more hopeful. You once called me a pessimist. I am, of course, but I am even more an optimist. As you know, much of my work has been with people who have problems which are often disturbing. One might believe that such experiences would lower my estimate of human nature. Instead, I find myself believing more and more strongly in the essential goodness of people and in their great possibilities.

At the same time, I am becoming continuously more pessimistic about the ideas and philosophies which people have accepted, especially in recent years. People are not so bad, their ideologies are bad. Individuals are not so weak; false ideas and ideals have robbed them of their strength. I find that most individuals are definitely superior to the education and the ideas that have been thrust upon them. Which reminds me that you asked what my book would be about. I can give you some idea by quoting one sentence: "The most interesting thing about the psychology of recent years is its rediscovery of man and the powers of which he is capable when his mind has been freed from the prevailing fallacies about himself."

Psychology, hardly a hundred years old as a science, is emerging from its *awkward* stage. During the past twenty-five years its discoveries about human nature have been

vii

truly amazing. Above all, psychology has discovered personality, that is, its nature, its importance, and how it may be developed. The discovery of personality has led to what is virtually a rediscovery of man himself. Man is now revealed as a creature of far greater possibilities than have usually been ascribed to him in recent years. He is revealed as a being infinitely superior to the pessimistic concepts of man now so popular. Even the processes by which he may develop his potentialities are now better understood.

I can almost hear you say: "That may be fine for individuals but what's the good of encouraging individuals when the world itself is going to pieces?"

I know, Frank, that this very thought is hampering many people today. But until we understand personality we cannot understand or remedy the ills of society. For three hundred years now, mind and knowledge have been developed at the expense of personality. It is roughly three hundred years since science said, in effect: The search for truth is the province of science, the search for personality and character is the province of the Church; therefore, let the Church take care of the rules of living, of personality; science will take care of the rules of thinking, of knowledge, of the mind.

The marvelous progress of science since that time is common knowledge. The world of things and ideas has been miraculously transformed.

There has been no corresponding development in the field of personality and character. Indeed, the development of the intellect has obscured all other aspects of the person. Modern civilization has created an almost complete vacuum in the place of personality and character. Educators and scientists, not to mention the Church, have been increasingly unable to define or develop personality. In the midst of great knowledge, man himself has become a great mystery.

No wonder that civilization is going to the dogs! No wonder that crazy social philosophies now tear individuals and nations apart! The most idealistic person undermines his own personality, and the altruistic reformer ruins personalities wholesale, by programs based on a false conception of human nature. Not until we understand personality can we appreciate the fallacies in so many of the current schemes of well-meaning dictators and reformers. Democracy, as I try to point out, can be understood only in terms of personality. Fascism, communism, social security, liberalism, and other social theories, can be evaluated only in terms of personality.

You see, Frank, personality to most psychologists is not just a sweet little mechanism by which one individual gets more than his share of sugar. This is the popular concept and a harmful one. Personality is at once a way of living and a philosophy of life. The discovery of personality, instead of implying a revolt against intellect, makes inevitable a higher level of intellectual achievement.

Yes, I am an optimist in the midst of pessimism. The popular pessimism becomes even a stimulus toward new and better visions of mankind. So you, Frank, will emerge from your retirement, I sincerely hope, more bitter toward false philosophies, but more hopeful about the people who have been misled by these fallacies to do you injury.

CONTENTS

I. THE REDISCOVERY OF MAN 3

II. WHAT IS PSYCHOLOGY? 29

III. THE PSYCHO-DYNAMICS OF PERSONALITY 55

IV. THE HABITS OF PERSONALITY 71

V. ON OVERCOMING FEARS AND WORRIES 93

VI. MACHINISTS OF THE SOUL 113

VII. PERSONAL SECURITY OR SOCIAL SECURITY? 135

VIII. THE PSYCHOLOGY OF SPORTSMANSHIP 157

IX. GOLD STANDARDS OF PERSONALITY 193
   The Psychology of Gold
   Will-Power
   Psychological Tests
   Progressive Standards
   Mental Telepathy
   Talk, Talk, Talk

X. SLAVERY OR PERSONALITY? 223
   The Steps into Bondage
   Fascism
   Democracy
   Communism

XI. THE PHILOSOPHY OF PERSONALITY 235

XII. THE SUPREME PERSONALITY 245

   APPENDIX 253

I

THE REDISCOVERY OF MAN

I

THE REDISCOVERY OF MAN

IN SEPTEMBER, 1936, a great tragedy occurred at Harvard University, a tragedy far more profound than the World War. And yet this tragedy, though its details were widely published and broadcast, passed almost unnoticed. It happened in connection with Harvard's celebration of its three hundredth year. The outstanding scholars of the world had been invited to present the contributions of their studies to mankind in a Tercentenary Conference of Arts and Sciences.

After two weeks of learned papers and discussion, the net conclusion, both stated and implied, was: that the physical sciences had made tremendous contributions to man's physical progress—the automobile, the X-ray, insulin, and thousands of other things; but that the social studies such as economics, history, anthropology, sociology, had contributed little or nothing to man's understanding of himself. While physics, chemistry, and biology had given man a miraculous control over his physical environment, they had added practically nothing to his control of his personal and social behavior. The printing press, the radio, had added in-

finitely to people's knowledge, little to their personalities. Though men were destined by medicine and
sanitation for a longer life, the frequency of mental illness was growing at an alarming rate. Individuals were
more at war with themselves, nations more liable to internal strife, and the world farther from international
peace than before.

This was the gist of Harvard's celebration of its three
hundredth year, and it might have been true of any of
our great universities. Add to this the fact that Harvard
was founded, like most of our historically great universities, by the religious leaders of the time, to prepare students "for public employment both in church and in
state," and the tragedy is complete. Three hundred years
of science and education, of emancipation from religion,
and to what end?

To the end that the true values of personality and character have been almost completely buried; that our educational system has become the most elaborate plan ever
devised for obscuring the obvious and homely facts of
life. To the end that we have created a complex system
of ideas which, instead of helping mankind, threatens,
like a parasitic growth, to kill the very civilization which
has produced it. A scientist like Alexis Carrel can write
a book on *Man the Unknown*, not because man is unknown, but because science has dismembered him almost
beyond recognition!

When I was in college the traditional questionnaire
for seniors included this item: "What is the greatest
thing you have gotten while in college?" In my day, the
majority of seniors usually answered, *friendships*, with

learning or *knowledge* a poor second. I can still remember the ridicule aimed at the barbaric students on whom four years of higher education had made so little impression that they could value friendships above culture! Then, and even more so in the twenty-five years since, the mind was supposed to require systematic cultivation, whereas friendships took care of themselves.

It is not surprising, therefore, that Dale Carnegie's book on *How to Win Friends and Influence People* has won such a tremendous audience. The very fact that it describes simple and obvious techniques of friendship makes it important because our civilization has so thoroughly ignored these values. Moreover, though these techniques may be simple in theory they are not easy in practice. And though their purpose may seem selfish their effect is to create habits of unselfishness. Mr. Carnegie's message may not be academically intellectual but it is profound. The winning of friends is truly the deepest concern of the world today. Neither peace nor prosperity can come except through more universal friendship and better personalities.

In the meanwhile, the multiplicities of science and education keep people artificially at odds, and conceal man's higher potentialities. War, once inevitable because of the simple greeds and passions of men, is now twice inevitable because of the false philosophies created by man's intellectual progress. With many high-sounding theories men have disguised their elemental passions, even glorified them and multiplied their range of expression.

Revolution and civil warfare were once the impulsive

result of economic desperation or tyranny; now, even in these democratic United States, strife is being systematically created by pressure groups and their conflicting theories of social justice. Abstract ideas rather than personal passions, lines of thought rather than bread-lines, are pushing this country toward violence.

Personal tragedy and defeat were once due to the individual's weakness or to physical circumstances beyond his control; today, with untold material advantages, even the most promising person is hamstrung by a formidable array of scientific and pseudo-scientific theories. These theories begin to operate against him even before he is born, and beset him to the last.

Friends to whom I have sometimes made these statements have asked: "Are you not exaggerating the effects of ideas, particularly their effect on the behavior of the less educated people?" Let us answer with examples of statements we may hear almost any day, and which are even embodied in the practice of social institutions.

"Personality is something you either have or don't have. It's a form of magnetism, a chemistry of charm, a physiology of the glands." Many parents have repeated this idea in explanation of their children and many young people have accepted this theory and acted accordingly, to their detriment. More significant still is the fact that almost our entire educational system, while assuming that it can improve the mind, tacitly assumes that it cannot improve the personality. Such efforts in behalf of personality as are now made are highly incidental to the chief purpose, which is to improve the intellect.

"His I.Q. (intelligence quotient) is low. He will

never do well in his studies." Any parent or educator, and, even at this late day, some psychologists, might make this statement. Here is a legitimate scientific device whose effectiveness has been curtailed by the addition of a theory which undermines the confidence of parents, of children, even of the schools, in the possibilities of training a mind. The ramifications of this theory are nation-wide.

"My child has no head for figures. It just seems impossible to teach her arithmetic." This belief, common not only to parents but to teachers, and so to the children themselves, is a simple version of the theory that heredity is the predominant influence in limiting mental growth.

"My child has a nervous disposition and must be handled accordingly." Many adults can attribute their present neuroticism to this belief of their parents and the treatment induced by this theory.

"I should like to have some tests to discover my aptitudes." Multitudes of people have been encouraged, by pseudo-psychologists and the popularizers of psychology, to regard such tests as the great solution of their vocational difficulties. By a simple mechanical device people now hope to discover some hidden spring or power which will automatically set them on the road to success. The old-fashioned fortune-teller and the confidence man, by adopting a few of the devices of psychology, have assumed a new respectability and won a tremendous following among a machine-minded public looking for short-cuts to success.

"A happy marriage depends upon finding a person who is physically or chemically compatible." This concept of compatibility has wrecked many marriages because it encourages the individual to deny his responsibility for creating compatibility by attributing it to the realm of biology and physiology. The divorce laws clearly reflect this concept. The theory of the frigid wife or husband is another aspect of this mechanistic influence.

"He suffers from an inferiority complex." How many people have said this of others, even of themselves, as though a sense of inferiority were a disease which in some mysterious way overtook the individual and rendered him helpless.

We could go on indefinitely with illustrations of this kind, representing widely accepted beliefs about human nature, beliefs which concretely influence a person's actions and the actions of society. The gist of these beliefs is this: that the individual is a victim of forces beyond his control; that his make-up and abilities are determined by heredity, or by accident, or by circumstance; that his happiness is dependent upon conditions outside himself; that there is less and less which he can do about these matters. Indeed, the more he learns about the world, the more numerous the forces of which he finds himself a victim, and the more numerous his excuses for dependence or despair.

This concept or misconcept of man has been in the active making for just about three hundred years. All the sciences have contributed toward its elaboration. Physics and chemistry, for example, have given us a mechanistic concept of the universe. The world is a machine, operating by immutable laws of cause and effect. Man is but a cog in this machine. Biology, except for men like Driesch, Jennings, and Sherrington, repeats much the same story. Man is a physical organism whose behavior is determined by heredity and by internal bits of machinery. A Jacques Loeb, discovering certain of these mechanisms, which he calls tropisms, concludes that all life is a collection of tropisms; that man—his fears, his hopes, his mistakes, his aspirations—is merely the interaction of myriad tropisms.

Astronomy reveals an infinite universe of wheels within wheels, held together by the forces of gravity. In this universe of astronomy man is an infinitesimal dot of little consequence. Geology and evolution portray him as little more than a monkey.

Endocrinology, discovering the glands, tells us an elaborate story of *The Glands Regulating Personality.* Hardly a medical convention goes by without announcements that the types of personality, the cycloid, the epileptoid, the schizophrenic, etc., are inherited through glandular structures, and there is little the individual can do for himself. In England a psychiatrist was knighted for his extensive writings, which, summed up, stated that drunkenness, phobias, hysterias, and the common mental ailings, were sicknesses brought about by the pressures and tensions of modern civilization. Such ailments, he maintained, were *not* the results of a person's sins against himself and society; they were phenomena for which the individual himself was not responsible. A psychiatrist connected with one of our great theological schools makes much the same claim, and it characterizes a large part of the psychiatric profession.

Certain psychologists, also, have maintained that behavior is purely mechanical, nothing more than automatic reflexes of cause and effect. Intelligence, as measured by the I.Q., some have insisted, is inherited and not subject to improvement. The poor child, they say, who inherits a low intelligence is to be pitied because not much can be done to raise his I.Q.

Finally, all people are to be pitied because their behavior is controlled by an unconscious mind as created by Freud and the psychoanalysts.

Every science and near science has added support to the conclusion that man is the victim of circumstance; that he is a small cog in a big machine; that he is a predetermined machine which can be kept running only by this tinkerer and that; in short, that he is anything but the master of his fate or the captain of his soul. The Calvinistic doctrine of predestination and the fatalism of the Stoics and of Oriental religions did not stifle man's spirit; indeed, they often gave men a rendezvous with fate which called forth their utmost powers and courage. The fatalism of our times is not the fatalism of faith but the fatalism of despair, it is not the product of the spirit but the creation of the mind. The sciences, the colleges and universities, our popular literature, have woven its tentacles through all aspects of our thinking. Our everyday vocabulary has become one of intellectual superstitions and scientific recipes for defeat.

This degrading concept of man reaches its climax in the teachings of our social studies, economics, sociology, political science, anthropology. Men and women, these studies assert with confidence, are the victims of their economic environment. They are helpless in the clutches of a soulless economic system. According to many students of society there is little or nothing individuals can do for themselves against these great odds. Only by changing the broad social mechanisms—by discarding the gold standard and inflating the dollar, by substituting government debts for private debts, or a planned economy for a free economy, or socialism for democracy, or communism for capitalism—only by such wholesale mechanistic devices can the majority of men achieve the abundant life. The popular manifestations of this social fatalism include such beliefs as:

The average of the average man can be raised only by changing the system.

Social security depends on old age pensions and unemployment insurance from a benevolent government, and not on the character and competence of the individual or his family.

Future depressions and wars can be avoided only by passing new laws.

The United States will continue to have about five million unemployed and a large portion of these will remain unemployable even if jobs are available. They can only be dealt with by wholesale schemes.

Weak characters and personalities are the result of being underprivileged. Only by raising the incomes of the less privileged can their morals and personalities be improved.

The frontiers of America are gone. There are no more opportunities for a man or a family to pioneer a new life.

Crime is the result of poverty. If we eliminate poverty, we shall have eliminated a large part of crime.

These are but a few of the many popular beliefs representing the mechanistic concept of man and society. If this concept were peculiar to the poor and the needy, it would not be so amazing; but it has been most highly developed among our intellectuals, among the well-educated, the comparatively well-to-do. From this group emanate those great schemes which treat people as puppets. Many of these schemes are high-minded and are pushed with good intentions, but they are nevertheless based on the assumption that people cannot be led or encouraged to help themselves, therefore they must be taken care of like cattle by some great, automatic social plan. This is the foundation for fascism both as it exists abroad and as it is being prepared by the organized social trends in America. The predominant scientific and social philosophy of our age is that man as an individual is helpless, a creature without self-respect, without will power, without faith in himself.

This definition of man, psychologists are finding, is not only horribly degrading but fundamentally untrue. To me, the most interesting thing about the psychology of recent years is its rediscovery of man and the powers of which he is capable when his mind has been freed from the prevailing fallacies about himself. Step by step, psychological studies are exposing the false ideas which man has developed both about himself and his world.

Thus man is now revealed as a being far greater than either the theories or the machines he has created. He is revealed as still the potential creator rather than the victim of his creations. He is a creature of free will and untold possibilities, not the slave of environment or circumstance. His capabilities are limited not so much by heredity and poverty as by his own vision of himself.

Personality, for example, is discovered to be not an accidental gift but an achievement. It is the result of certain habits which can be acquired only by practice. Whatever the glandular heredity, the child who practices the desirable habits will develop a better personality than the child who fails to practice such habits. Even in small things this truth is demonstrated. Our studies show that children who often attribute their failures to hard luck tend to have poorer personalities than do those who blame themselves. The former regard themselves as victims, the latter believe that they can do something to improve their success. We find that children who often say, "I can't do this," or "I can't help it," tend to have poorer personalities than those who will not admit permanent defeat. The latter refuse to accept their fate or clumsiness but keep on trying.

The parent who believes that his child has inherited no gift for arithmetic encourages the child in the same belief. The defeatist attitude thus set up makes it more difficult for the child to develop what talent he has. Psychologists are continually taking such cases in hand and confounding parents and teachers with the results.

The more thorough studies of the I.Q. show that the I.Q. is not stationary except in terms of the averages for many children. The high I.Q. of a brilliant child may fall through neglect or laziness, while the naturally less brilliant child may raise his I.Q. through consistent effort and application. In fact, the whole trend of scientific psychological studies in recent years has been toward establishing the small influence of heredity as compared with the powerful influence of development and training.

Aptitudes, we find, are not little reservoirs of talent just waiting to be discovered, when they will gush out in their full richness. Whatever the aptitudes of an individual, they will amount to little unless the individual will devote years of hard work and self-discipline to their development. Again and again we find people whose failure must be attributed to an excess of aptitudes, no one of which they have systematically cultivated. Nature, or a mechanical universe, will not develop inherent aptitudes. The person who makes the most of little or no special talent is better off than the person rich in talents who trains none to perfection.

In short, the difference between success and failure is essentially a matter of philosophies. A philosophy of failure makes failure inevitable even with the most richly endowed person; and a philosophy of success can do miracles with one poorly endowed. And yet, though man is free to choose either, one being true and the other false, he has chosen the false philosophy.

We give our children today a vocabulary of defeat, ready made. The mere term *phobia* practically doubles a fear. Its use often creates a fear where none existed before or transforms a mild fear into one more serious. I have often wished that the term *inferiority complex* had never been coined, because then millions of people would not even know they had an inferiority complex. There would be one less manufactured idea for them to fear. In my work with people I never use such terms because, in the first place, they obscure rather than illuminate a problem, and, in the second place, they only add to the destructive ideas already at work. The fears which people generate without assistance are bad enough without multiplying them through a psychiatric and psychoanalytic vocabulary.

We are not saying here that *ignorance is bliss* but that half baked theories add unnecessary misery.

A sense of inferiority, we find, is not a disease. I have told hundreds of complaining parents: "You should be thankful that your child has a sense of inferiority. The children to worry about are those who always think they are smart, who know better than their elders, who see no reason for painful practice or humble effort. The child, however, who feels inferior can usually be trained to develop abilities which in time will make him truly superior. All genuine superiority grows out of a sense of inferiority. The person who admits his inferiority and then does something about it, develops superiority."

Here, most dramatically, we see the difference between the mechanistic and the psychological concept of man. On the one hand there are those who are inferior and refuse to recognize their inferiority or believe that there is nothing which they can do to become superior. In their extreme forms, these individuals are often radicals and reformers. Since they will not take steps to improve themselves, they want to reform the entire system. They cannot see that in any scheme of life whatsoever, they would probably be misfits unless they changed themselves. On the other hand are those people who believe that they *can* develop their personalities and that only what they do with themselves will result in their achievement of competence and superiority. These are the people who, after the shouting and shooting are over, sustain any form of society, whether it be democracy or communism.

A young man, typical of many, described himself as having an inferiority complex. He traced for us the history of its development. His mother had babied him as a child. When the boys treated him roughly she sheltered him. When he had not prepared his lessons and said he felt too ill to go to school, his mother kept him at home and made a fuss over his health. When he wanted some elaborate toy, she gave him the money. When he grew older and had difficulty finding or holding a job and blamed his employer or the depression, his mother sympathized. In short, his home environment had given him this complex, and here he was, a failure as compared with his friends. Now his mother had lost a substantial part of her income and his only hope for the future was a well-to-do relative who was not yet ready to die.

The psychologist, confronted with this situation, would have to say in substance: "You seem to have analyzed the causes of your condition quite well, up to a point. You have been the victim of the environment you describe. However, you have missed the most important point, which is that, with your education and privileges, you have permitted yourself to remain the victim. If you continue to depend on the future, if a relative should leave you a million dollars, you will still be a victim. No amount of money can make you happy or superior. You can achieve superiority only by acting from now on as though you had nothing but yourself to fall back on. Such a program of action as we may suggest you alone can adopt and execute. Once you adopt this program you must act always as though it were impossible to fail, even though it takes you years to succeed."

So many of the individuals who come to a psychologist with their failures are able to describe in detail the causes of their difficulties: the family had lost its money or never had any money; the father had been too indulgent or too strict; the mother had been too easy or too domineering; they were the victims of a mother- or a father-fixation; they had tried many vocations but none had proved interesting; etc., without end. Often these individuals have read a good deal of what they thought was psychology, so that they can describe their difficulties in terms of phobias, an Oedipus complex, rationalization, projection, over-compensation, inhibitions, and many other notions of the psychoanalytic school.

In such situations our answer usually is: "Let us assume that your analysis of the causes of your failure is substantially correct, and that you have been the victim of these outside forces in your environment. The one important question now is: What are *you* going to *do?* The only person in the world who can solve this problem is you. We may help you to map out a plan of action, but only you can carry this plan into effect. Only you can assume the responsibility for its success. The more time we spend analyzing the causes, which are in the past, the less time and power you will have to practice the new habits and skills which you need to take you out of this situation. The time for talk has ended. From now on the emphasis must be on action, struggle, painful practice, embarrassing moments, self-sacrifice, discipline, patient and persistent effort."

It is remarkable how this challenge to the individual's powers of self-determination and capacity for effort stimulates many to a new attack on life. The tragedy is that for so many years our civilization and its educational forces have permitted them to believe in their own helplessness. Worse still, it has supplied them with a collection of intellectual tools by which to build a tower of logic in defense of their failures.

Here are the concluding sentences from a written statement by a high school graduate in which he gives many details from his childhood and adolescence to account for his present unhappy state. "I have become concious of a sense of finality in all things relating to my existence. It seems as if there were many fixed and arbitrary forces making all things appear changless and permanent. I am beset with phobias and inhibitions. A sense of dissatisfaction and loss of confidence literally dog my footsteps. My job is far from congenial, yet though I know or think I know what I do not like to do, that which I would like to do is hidden from my gaze like a thick fog." This young man could even spell the modern vocabulary of defeat better than the vocabulary of success based on proper training in school.

People sometimes tell us: "Your work with so many abnormal and misshapen personalities is bound to give you a distorted viewpoint of human nature and its work-ings." As a matter of fact, more than ninety percent of our work is with normal people or people who would be regarded as normal by all accepted criteria. Our atten-tion to more extreme cases is necessary for the light they throw on the proper development of the normal individual. Moreover, our studies of personality among many thousands of school children throughout the United States, most of whom would be regarded as normal, are aimed at the prevention of abnormality rather than at its cure. This is the program of most psychologists working in the field of personality.

An example of a quite normal kind but highly sig-nificant of a prevailing social misconcept of man is rep-resented by the following letter from an eighteen year-old boy: "When I was sixteen years old, my father died and left me the only support of my mother. I had to give up high school and go to work. For two years I have been supporting us both and taking some high school work at night. My mother would like to work but her health will not permit. The going has been tough. My ambition is to be an engineer but at the pres-ent rate the outcome is uncertain. Recently I learned that it would be possible for my mother to go on relief and for me to get aid enough to go to an engineering school full time. Some of my friends have told me I would be foolish not to take it. Even my mother favors it for my sake. What would you advise? I am very am-bitious and want to succeed."

My reply to him was: "You have the most priceless ingredient of success in the world, namely, self-dependence. In an age when children are all too willing to depend on their families and families to depend on others, you have courageously struck out for yourself. You have the stuff that makes men great. As soon as you accept help from an outside source you sacrifice your intellectual and moral independence unless you can do it through a business-like loan or a scholarship based on merit. An engineering education obtained in this way, in my opinion, will not do nearly so much for your success as will the attempt to obtain such an education independently. I congratulate you on your difficult situation and your independence thus far. As you value your personality, your happiness, your success, hold fast to this priceless ingredient. Do not sell it for a mess of pottage."

Whereas our civilization has created the philosophy of defeat it has at the same time developed intellects whose arrogance knows no bounds. Such minds take this philosophy, false as it is, as a lever by which to move the world. The term "brain trust" has been appropriately used to describe them.

Whereas millions of people are still struggling to improve themselves these confident minds now say: "Your struggles are useless; we shall arrange matters for you."

Whereas millions are still striving to plan their own economy, these superintellectuals now claim: "Your individual or group efforts are beside the point; what all of you have failed to solve, we will solve through a single planned economy."

Whereas farmers have been struggling for years with nature and the laws of supply and demand, these supermen assert: "Your efforts are futile; we have a plan which will automatically take care of these matters for you."

Whereas employers and employees, with the faults and virtues common to both, have been striving to create teamwork in a common interest, these intellectual machinists of the soul proclaim: "Society must be divided into warring classes; here is a set of laws to govern this warfare."

The ambitiousness of the plans thus offered is in direct proportion to the confidence of their proponents in the philosophy of mechanism. Such leaders, while protesting pity for the poor, have a supreme contempt for the characters and personalities of individuals and a naïve or arrogant faith in social-economic schemes. They are the ultimate expression of an intellectual civilization, which substitutes ideas for experience, abstractions for reality, and scientific fictions for man himself.

The antithesis of this philosophy of defeat and its confidence in wholesale schemes is not a social policy of *laissez-faire*. Whereas the social planning of our time treats people largely as permanent weaklings, the social efforts suggested by the findings of psychology will treat people as self-reliant individuals, at least potentially. *Social movements toward a more abundant life need not degrade personalities. Liberal thinking does not have to be loose thinking.* The great leaders and liberators of history were men and women who inspired their followers to a fuller life through struggle, privation, and personal achievement.

Moses delivered the people of Israel out of Egypt and

led them into a land of milk and honey, but only through an epic of starvation, thirst, and self-discipline. The leaders of our day achieve popularity because, from their easy chairs, they promise the multitude sitting in comfort before their radios, a life of abundance for the simple effort of walking to the voting booth. Nero fiddled while Rome burned. *Our popular leaders sing sweet songs while the characters of a nation crumble. Their tune is: "You do not need better personalities, you have me! You do not require stronger characters, I will give you the abundant life!"*

This wet-nurse leadership is not an accident. It is not an incident peculiar to any one man or political party. It is the inevitable result of three hundred years of physical science and mis-education, the central theme of which is the concept of man as a helpless cog in a mechanistic universe. In everyday experience this development has manifested itself among parents in their increasing tendency to treat their children as helpless, as requiring prolonged subsidies. The result among children has been an attitude expressed in the phrase: "Let father do it. Let father give me an allowance. Let father give me an education. Let father give me the use of an automobile. Let my family take the responsibility while I take the liberties."

It manifests itself among adults toward their neighbors as follows: "Let the city take care of social evils and unemployment." Among the cities, the cry has been: "Let the state take care of its people." The states have increasingly said: "Let the Federal Government take care of our citizens on relief, of economic problems, labor disputes, law-enforcement, local public improvements." Step by step, individuals have denied their independence and have pushed their responsibilities farther away.

The hue and cry in recent years has been about the rights and liberties of American citizens; less and less has been heard about their responsibilities, which alone make rights and liberties possible. With some exceptions rich and poor alike, Christian and pagan, educated and ignorant, have delegated their moral and economic independence to others, and have accepted the role of victim or beneficiary. *The result, as history will in my opinion show, is the most wholesale degradation of character and personality which the world has ever seen, and among privileged and so-called underprivileged alike.*

Aside from religion and the discoveries of psychology, the true concept of man, strange to say, has survived in the literature of fiction. At this writing the novel, *Gone With the Wind*, has been purchased by a million and a half people and read, probably, by ten million. Why? Many have asked this question. The explanation may be this: Scarlett, though in many ways not an admirable person, was a woman who remained forever the master of her world rather than its victim. Neither war, nor disappointment in love, nor scandal, nor starvation, nor the burning of her home, nor the pain of childbirth, nor bloodshed, none of these catastrophes could daunt her spirit. Here was a woman who experienced in a short lifetime more tragedies than most people ever dream, who rushed to meet disaster, and emerged with courage unimpaired. Here was a woman who, to millions suffering the comparative luxuries of a depression today, exemplified a personal triumph over social insecurity. Ten million readers! Ten million nostalgic gasps from the victims of a machine concept of social security, a people still faintly protesting against the loss of their personal responsibility and power.

At the same time another novel, *Drums Along the Mohawk*, was a good second in popularity, and for the same reason. Here is a story of the hardships of early settlers in the Mohawk Valley, the loss of their homes and farms, the massacres by Indians and their white allies, the breaking up of families, a central government which taxed without pity, yet gave no protection in return, a story of the triumph of people over themselves and their environment.

In the literature of fiction, read for pleasure, the true definition of man still occasionally survives; whereas the literature of science and sociology, read for education, increasingly annihilates the spirit of man. Now for the first time a quantitative science, psychology, denies the trend of all earlier science in respect to the definition of human nature; exposes the fallacies in the by-products of these sciences; reaffirms the integrity of man and his final authority over all his intellectual creations; extends hope and reassurance to the individual and to a society seeking the road to personality and happiness.

A great astronomer once remarked to a friend: "To the astronomer, man is an infinitesimal dot in an infinite universe." "Ah!" said his friend, "but man is still the astronomer." Just so psychology reverses the emphasis from a study of the macrocosm, the universe at large, to the study of the microcosm, that is man himself; and by revealing the true nature of the individual also reveals the only foundation on which any social order may safely build.

II

WHAT IS PSYCHOLOGY?

II.

WHAT IS PSYCHOLOGY?

PSYCHOLOGY is essentially the scientific study of habits and their formation, first, so that those habits may be better understood, second, so that they may be better controlled. Upon hearing this definition people often ask: "But where does the mind come in? I thought psychology was the study of the mind." My response to this natural question is usually: "True, but did you ever hear of a child being born with the multiplication table or the *a b c*'s already in his mind? These are habits, and no matter how good a child's heredity, no matter how high his capacity at birth, these habits like most habits can be acquired only through practice, imitation, and discipline."

Every new parent sees a mind in the making where only the capacity for a mind existed before—the habit of saying *mama* and *daddy*, of counting from one to twenty, of reading and writing, of repeating the multiplication table, and so on through childhood and adolescence. These habits, and thousands more acquired by practice, make a mind, and without them there is no mind. Without them there is no thinking, no reasoning; for they are the tools of reason. A mind without an

29

adequate collection of habits is like a shop without the necessary machines—its product is limited, its thinking and conclusions are one-sided or incomplete.

An attractive young woman came to us one day with this request: "I want you to straighten out my mind." She then proceeded to tell us about her mental difficulties, and revealed a mind truly appalling in its confusion. Upon inquiring into the details of her life, it appeared that she had left her home in a small city and come to New York where she had obtained a job and for two years supported herself. Evidently she had acquired many good habits. She did not, however, associate with her fellow employees at the office, she had made no friends there, she lived in a room alone and usually ate alone, she spent most of her spare time in reading, going to lectures, and what she called "improving her mind". The evidence showed that her loneliness was due not to the isolation of a large city but to her failure to acquire the habits of social living in her youth.

When we suggested that she get a room in a women's club such as the Y.W.C.A., spend several evenings a week in some of its group activities, including athletic games, and invite some of her fellow employees to have luncheon with her occasionally, she exclaimed: "But I don't want to do those things! I don't like them! I want you to straighten out my mind." Whereupon we were compelled to tell her: "Unless you first straighten out some of your habits, neither we nor anybody else can straighten out your mind. Your thinking is confused and unbalanced because you have failed to acquire some of the most important habits in life, that is, habits of dealing with a sufficient variety of people in common situations. Such habits are necessary tools for balanced thinking."

"But," she objected, "isn't it true that many great minds have developed without these petty social habits which you call important?" Here was a question, which, in one form or another, has been asked by many people. Undoubtedly some of the great minds of history have developed despite the lack of adequate social habits. Such minds, however, have usually achieved greatness through their concentration in some specialized field such as music, physics, electricity—fields in which they became creative. Great in their chosen field, these minds have often been notorious for their lack of balance in other fields. For every person who achieves greatness in this way, there are probably hundreds of thousands who, through the lack of adequate habits, as in the case of this young woman, achieve only misery and intellectual futility.

Creative genius may be justified at any cost, but psychology is concerned first of all with the habits which most of us need in order to have reasonably good minds. The parents of this young woman, like so many others, had not understood nor insisted on the development of certain important habits by their daughter. They are not to be too severely judged because, in our present civilization, we do not even know which habits are important and which are not. Many of the habits considered supremely important today are probably least important, and vice-versa.

Many mothers have lamented to me: "My boy simply will not sit down and read a good book. He is always outside playing baseball with the boys, or practicing his tennis, or doing something with his friends." To such well-meaning mothers my answer has usually been: "You ought to be thankful for that kind of boy, so long as his activities are largely athletic and wholesome, and he does the required work in school. If, in his youth, he acquires the habits of getting along with and understanding people in the flesh, the people in books which he will read as he grows older will mean infinitely more to him."

During the past fifteen or twenty years especially, psychology has made tremendous progress in discovering the habits which make for a good mind and a good personality. Many of these discoveries are merely a reaffirmation of truths about human nature uttered centuries ago; but in these days of educated confusion and subsidized chaos, the confirmation of ancient truths has all the merit of originality. If anything, rediscovery is more important than discovery, since the general trend of our time is to repudiate all that is old and place credence in all that is new. "We are living in a new social order, where change is the rule; our oxcart ideas must give way to streamlined ideas, keeping pace with our fast-moving age." So runs the bromide of the day. And yet, when psychologists, with scientific thoroughness, investigate widely accepted streamlined theories, they are often found to be fallacious or inadequate.

The emotional life is one field in which this is particularly true. Here a whole library of modern psychiatric and psychoanalytic theories, foreign to psychology, have come into popular acceptance. A mother once discussed with us the problem of her twelve-year-old son.

For years this boy had been given to violent temper tantrums, during which he would smash his toys, throw them at the walls, scream and swear at his mother, do violence to anything within his reach. And yet he loved his mother, did not want to go away to camp or to school; he wanted to stay at home. Inquiry revealed that this boy was doing very well in his studies, was an outstanding athlete in his class, was popular with his classmates and well liked by his teachers, had several hobbies in which he showed a keen, creative interest. In fact, he was a boy far above the average in all-round habits and skills.

"Does he lose his temper and have tantrums at school or among his playmates?" we inquired.

"No," replied the mother, "so far as I know, they occur only at home."

Since the boy had a little sister, it would have been simple to follow the psychoanalytic clichés and ascribe the brother's tantrums to his jealousy of the sister as a rival for the mother's attentions. Our inquiries, however, showed that his mother had been a voracious reader of books on psychology—or rather what she thought were books on psychology. From them she had concluded that a child should be allowed to express himself freely, that he should never be given corporal punishment, that he should be reasoned with rather than disciplined. Through the application of these theories, which most psychologists have never accepted, she had systematically cultivated in her son the habit of throwing tantrums. His temper spells were a specific emotional habit, which operated only toward the mother, and not toward the rest of the world which would neither tolerate this habit nor prolong it by talk or reasoning.

The development of the common habits, like writing, adding, spelling, etc., is readily understood by most people. There is no question, for example, that in spelling words correctly we must acquire a thousand or maybe five thousand habits, each word a separate habit. But in respect to the feelings, the emotions of anger, fear, hate, love, greed, sympathy, etc., the importance of habit formation is not nearly so well understood. And yet, the emotions are developed through habit just as are the habits of spelling, walking, eating, and talking.

Just as the child is born without the multiplication table in its mind, so he is born without habits of emotional response. The emotions grow out of the energy which the body generates from its meals and rest. At first this energy is chaotic and explosive, but gradually we acquire the specific habit patterns by which to control and express it. We develop definite habits of temper, sometimes good, sometimes not so good as in the case of the boy just described. We develop habits of pleasure and displeasure. The child develops the habits of affection for his parents or nurse, or for his mother by adoption, if that be the case. He may develop fear of the dark, a wholly acquired habit or an experience confirmed by habit. The child acquires likes and sometimes strong dislikes for certain kinds of foods. Elaborate emotional habits often grow up around these likes and dislikes.

One day, while driving with a young couple and their three-year-old son, the mother who was driving braked the car sharply, causing the child, who was standing between the father's knees, to pitch forward and bump his head smartly against the instrument board. The father let out a roar of laughter, picked up the boy, and exclaimed: "My, that was a good bump! Look what you hit!" and with elaborate motions he pointed out the exact spot. The mother, helpless at the moment, looked daggers at the father, but the child, who had drawn his breath for a loud wail, had relaxed and was quietly examining the instrument board. Some minutes later he abstractedly felt his forehead where a considerable welt now showed. The mother looked at the father and smiled. Parents are directly responsible for the emotional habits formed by their children. By misdirecting the impulses of their children in respect to eating, going to bed, playing, talking, and hundreds of other details, they foster the very habits which later become emotional problems.

The development of the emotions through life continues in the same fashion of habit patterns. Some people habitually go into ecstasy at the sight of a beautiful sunset, some at the sight of a well-broiled steak. Some thrill to the fragrance of an exotic perfume, others are disgusted by the same odor. To be sure, the energy or emotional capacities of individuals differ by nature, and no matter what the common elements of training or environment, individual differences will appear. Yet, in certain basic respects, emotional energies are the same.

After puberty, the tremendous energies of sex come into full play. These energies are capable of being transformed into an infinite variety of habits and skills only indirectly related to sex. If adequate skills and habits have been developed in childhood, the wholesome development of the sex energies into habit patterns centered about a family becomes highly probable. The popular belief that a happy marriage depends on finding an "affinity," a physical compatibility of the emotions, is a conspicuous example of the modern fallacies regarding the emotional life. Happiness in marriage depends primarily on a multitude of habits acquired before marriage rather than on the simple emotions of sex.

The case of the boy who had been allowed to develop temper tantrums toward his mother is typical of thousands of emotional habits which have come under our observation. Adults may not throw dishes or deface the walls—their tantrums usually take on more refined forms. The young woman who exclaimed: "But I don't want to do those things! I don't like them!" was able to weave elaborate reasons around her stubborn likes and dislikes. The more unbalanced or inadequate a person's habits are, the more vehement and elaborate usually is his reasoning to justify that condition. This is especially true of educated and well-read people. By book and chapter they can prove their point. Seldom do people realize that their logic is governed by their habits, and if their habits are wrong, their reasoning is bound to be crooked.

"What we need in the present situation," writes a woman about a popular social issue, "is facts, and more facts." Yet, from the tone of her writing, it was perfectly obvious that the more facts she had the more good reasons she would give for her bad thinking. Never before has the world had so many facts so widely distributed, and yet our thinking about personal and social matters seems more chaotic and contradictory as time goes on. The person who does not acquire, through example, authority, and discipline, a well-balanced set of habits in youth, is bound to think crookedly as he matures.

The conclusions of modern psychology in respect to habits confirm the conclusions of Plato and Aristotle arrived at over two thousand years ago. "Now it is clear that in education," says Aristotle, "habit must go before reason and the body before the mind. . . . We get the virtues by first having performed the energies, as is the case also in all the other arts. . . . By doing just actions we become just, by performing temperate actions, temperate, and by performing brave actions we become brave. . . . In a word, the habits are produced out of similar energies; therefore the energies we perform must be of a certain character; for the differences in the habits create corresponding differences in the energies. . . . Therefore it is necessary to be trained immediately from childhood, so Plato says, to feel pleasures and pains at proper objects, for this is right education. . . . It does not therefore make a slight, but an important, nay, the whole difference, whether we have been brought up in the right habits or the wrong habits from childhood. . . . If arguments and theories were able by themselves to make people good, they would, in the words of Theognis, be entitled to receive high and great rewards, and it is with theories that we should have to provide ourselves. But the truth apparently is that arguments and theories are incapable of converting the mass of men to goodness and beauty of character. . . . For he who lives in obedience to passion would not listen to reasoning which turns him from it; nay, more, he would not understand it."

These are the conclusions of pioneer psychologists who believed in the supremacy of reason and the cultivation of the mind, but who did not lose sight of the fundamentals.

"In men, reason and mind are the ends toward which nature strives," says Aristotle, but points out that children cannot reason properly until they have acquired the right habits; that these habits must therefore be inculcated by example and discipline, since to reason with children not yet equipped to reason is futile; that adults who have failed to acquire the right habits are bound to reason wrongly, and moreover, that they will not even recognize the fallaciousness of their reasoning.

There was something hopeful about the young woman who wanted her mind straightened out. The tragedy lies in the thousands of unhappy or unsuccessful people, many of them highly educated, with many positive opinions about themselves and about the world at large, who do not even suspect that their thinking is usually crooked. Still greater is the tragedy of people, very successful in one field, who, in the absence of well-balanced basic habits, reason incorrectly in every other field.

The issue raised by the presentation thus far is well expressed by this question, which many mothers have put to me: "If a child is miserable in athletic sports, should the parent insist on his participation?" My answer is usually a series of questions: "If a child is miserable in studying arithmetic or spelling, would you therefore excuse him from these studies? If he rebels at eating with a knife and fork, would you permit him to eat as he likes? If he hates school and has difficulties with the other children, would you allow him to give up school?"

The issue here is not one of compulsion or regimentation. There are already so many things in which we take authority and compulsion for granted that the true issue is: *What habits and habit-forming activities should be compulsory?* Conceivably, athletic sports and games should be as compulsory and as systematically taught in every year of the grade school as are reading, writing, and arithmetic. The progress of modern psychology lies in its discovery that many habits, which we have believed important, are relatively unimportant, and many which we have considered of incidental value, such as athletic sports and games, are supremely important in developing a sound mind and an effective personality.

Diametrically opposed to the wisdom of Plato and Aristotle, and to the concept of habit-formation here described, is the popular philosophy which encourages children and adults to substitute self-expression for discipline, and reason for authority. A fifteen-year-old girl, who was poor in her academic studies but showed signs of artistic talent, was examined by us with regard to her possibilities as an art student. She had been encouraged by her teachers and given wide latitude in her artistic efforts from an early grade on, possibly at the expense of learning to read and to write properly. The mother had carefully saved samples of her drawings and these samples revealed this interesting set of facts. First, nearly all her work had been done with colored crayons and watercolors; there were practically no drawings in pencil or in black and white. Second, her subjects were nearly all imaginative; there were practically no efforts to draw people, or objects, or settings from life. Third, while her pictures contained girls and women, there was an almost total absence of men. When asked why she did not draw men, her answer was that she found men too difficult to draw. In this respect, as well as in respect to simple objects, learning how to observe and reproduce line and form, shadow and light, and the elements of perspective, her work showed an almost total lack of direction and discipline.

For hours and years she had been expressing *herself*, without acquiring the habits and skills essential to expressing anything worth while. The praise of her work had even given her a false sense of security, since, if she entered an art school, she would have to begin with the very elements she had so far been permitted to avoid, and would have to draw what was assigned rather than what she preferred. Even with some artistic capacity, it was now doubtful whether this girl, after years of encouragement in self-expression, could survive the discipline of self-restraint and self-development.

The examination of adults, in so many instances, has revealed traces of talents which were now more reminiscent than hopeful. Often, especially in individuals with several aptitudes, the application of the principle of self-expression had led to a dissipation and distraction of these talents, when the arbitrary and consistent cultivation of one or two would have led to unusual achievement.

The subject of artistic and unusual aptitudes, while more romantic, is no more important than the subject of basic habits of a common kind. A boy of sixteen, who was about to be dismissed by one of the best preparatory schools for failure in his studies, was examined with the following test results:

Test Results

Scholastic capacity or general intelligence (Otis Advanced)[1]

    Excels 85% of high school students. I.Q. equivalent, 1.20

P.Q. or Personality Quotient (Link)

    P.Q. 1.20, or well above average

Mechanical aptitude (Stenquist Assembling)

    Well above the average for high school boys

Educational Achievements (Terman, New Stanford V)

Reading ability	equals average	at 17 years
Spelling	" "	at 13 years
Grammar	" "	at 15 years
Literature	" "	at 17 years
History and Civics	" "	at 15 years
Geography; Physiology	" "	at 16 years
Arithmetic Computation	" "	at 13 years
Arithmetic Reasoning	" "	at 14 years

Our comments on these results were, in part, as follows: "The tests show that —— has a high measure of scholastic capacity or general intelligence, but that he

[1] The names in parentheses specify the test and the psychologist who developed that test and whose norms are used.

has failed to acquire many of the basic habits in spelling and arithmetic. His low marks at school, especially in algebra and English, are probably due to the fact that, in the years before he entered preparatory school, he did not receive sufficient discipline or the right supervision in mastering the fundamentals of spelling, rhetoric, and arithmetic. Naturally, a boy who has not acquired the habits of short division will have difficulty with long division. Facility in the habits of adding, subtracting, multiplying, etc., can be gained only by routine drill and repetition. If he lacks many of these elementary habits, his ability in arithmetic reasoning or doing problems, as shown by our test, is naturally handicapped; and when he comes to algebra, he is still more at a loss. The same is true of his spelling and grammar, and their effects on his more advanced work in English.

"Therefore, we suggest that he drop algebra for the rest of this year, and be given a thorough overhauling in the routines of arithmetic, and also some extra drill in spelling and grammar. He should also be given some drill in how to study, since his study habits are evidently very superficial. Reading ten pages of history, for example, is not studying. He should be taught to read one paragraph, put the book aside, and then repeat to himself the facts contained in that paragraph.

"With the proper drill in these fundamental habits, he should be able within a year or so to do creditable work in all his subjects. His personality habits are splendid, and the boy is worth this extra attention, especially since the habit deficiencies shown by our tests are probably due to lack of adequate discipline at a time when he was too young to understand its necessity.

"We have explained the situation to him in terms of the simple mechanics of habit-formation and believe that he is ready to coöperate intelligently and energetically in the extra disciplines the school may now impose."

Within six months, all doubts of this boy's being able to remain at his school and do progressively better in his studies had disappeared. His case is typical of many illustrating the fact that no matter what a person's I.Q. or intelligence quotient, it avails little unless the necessary habit-routines are acquired through practice or discipline. There is little intelligence in spelling, quite the opposite; as soon as we begin to think or reason about our spelling, we are lost, and this is true of a great many mental operations which depend on practice. On the other hand, many a person not so well endowed with intelligence, by diligent application and work, cultivates a collection of habits which give him in the end a fine mind. Whatever a person's heredity or privileges, the critical question is: To what extent are the potentialities converted into sound habit-mechanisms? With our present theories and methods of education, the genius or exceptional child is more likely to be a problem case in the end than is the person with a moderately good mental capacity.

The above example illustrates, in a relatively simple case, how psychological tests are used to measure and give an inventory of a person's habits. The tests of capacities and aptitudes place emphasis on the measuring of those habits which the individual has acquired by himself, without extra pressure and drill. Educational and achievement tests emphasize those habits which the individual is supposed to acquire under the pressure of school discipline or special training. To the extent that we can accurately survey a person's habits we are nearer to an appraisal of his difficulties and their causes, and to an agreement on a plan of action for developing the right habits.

Another example of this use of tests is the case of a high school senior who had twice failed the College Entrance Board examinations in Latin and English. This was a serious matter to him and his family, since he hoped to enter Harvard and to take a liberal arts course in preparation for the ministry. Psychological tests given to this boy, whom we may refer to as Gilbert, gave the following results:

Test Results

Scholastic capacity or general intelligence (Otis norms)
  Excels 72% of college students
Personality Inventory (Bernreuter)
  Below average in personality traits
English Training—spelling, grammar, etc. (Iowa)
  Inferior to 63% of entering college freshmen
English Aptitude—reading, comprehension, etc. (Iowa)
  Inferior to 52% of entering college freshmen
Foreign Language Aptitude (Iowa)
  Inferior to 67% of entering college freshmen

Mathematics Training (Iowa)
  Superior to 83% of entering college freshmen
Mathematics Aptitude (Iowa)
  Superior to 95% of entering college freshmen
Mechanical Aptitude (Stenquist)
  Superior to 87% of adult army men
Mechanical Knowledge (O'Rourke)
  Superior to 90% of norms group
Spatial Perception (Link-Minnesota Form board)
  Superior to 90% of first year engineering students

The report on Gilbert's examination was, in part, as follows: "Whatever the reasons for Gilbert's low score in English and foreign language aptitude, his scores in mathematics and in the tests for mechanical skills show a high degree of aptitude in these fields. However, during his four years of high school, he has taken the minimum courses in mathematics, no physics or chemistry, no shopwork, but one course in mechanical drawing in which, as we should expect, he did extremely well. Why a boy with these aptitudes, and a deficiency in English which dates back to his grade school years, should have been given the additional handicap of four years of Latin, is hard to justify. Certainly the sciences are equal, as disciplines, to Latin, and, since both are optional, the choice of subjects which corresponds with aptitudes is desirable. If he had taken the scientific instead of the classical course, the present difficulty could have been largely avoided.

"As things are now, we can only suggest that, if Gilbert, by extra tutoring and special effort, does succeed in entering Harvard, he would do better to take an engineering or a scientific course rather than a liberal arts course. This plan would also be more conducive to developing his personality, which certainly does not point toward the ministry. Although a big, strong boy, he has been very unsocial in school and has not participated in the games, athletic sports, or group activities of the students. We have agreed with him on a program including tennis, soccer, bridge, and several other group activities, which will help him develop social skills and important personality habits. He has also agreed to take dancing lessons this Christmas vacation, an important step in acquiring habits of sex adjustment, which he has resisted so far. If he takes a scientific or engineering course, his laboratory work will compel him to work in pairs or groups, and this will help develop his personality habits. Only a boy whose personality habits are already well developed can take the more subjective studies of a liberal arts course with a minimum of risk."

Four years later this boy appeared again, but, though his weight had not increased a pound and his appearance was much the same, he was a different being. He had been a vegetable, now he was a personality, his energies were flowing outward. He had gotten into Harvard, he had taken the scientific course, he had done very well in mathematics, chemistry, physics, and biology, and his good work in these subjects had helped carry along the required language courses. He had followed the program of group activities and the results were obvious. Indeed, a repetition of the personality test given four years earlier showed these results:

	1931	1935
Extrovert habits	59	87
Habits of social initiative	10	41
Habits of self-sufficiency	30	83
Emotional stability	39	79

Now he had come to tell us that he had decided to go on with the study of medicine, an excellent choice, since the basic aptitudes for medicine and mechanical engineering are so much the same.

This example raises the question of an effective personality as distinguished from a good mind. Personality, as we shall see in subsequent chapters, is the result of habits formed exactly like the habits of reading and writing, that is, by practice.

Although the findings of psychology may prove that certain basic habits are desirable for all people, the record of Gilbert, which is highly typical, indicates a consideration for individuality which goes far beyond the existing thought and educational practice. As I have stated elsewhere, our present educational system is better equipped to give eight years of the wrong kind of education to its pupils than eight hours of competent psychological diagnosis calculated to help the individual in his choice of courses and schools.

Such examinations require from eight to twelve hours or more, including personal histories not given here, and possibly tests of musical, artistic, and other aptitudes or habits. There are now well over a thousand psychological tests, and such tests are the scientific devices by which psychologists study habits, their formation, and their consequences. These tests are to psychology what the blood-pressure test, X-ray, blood-count, etc., are to medicine; what the scales, thermostat, graduated glass, etc., are to chemistry; what the transit, chain, and logarithms are to the surveyor; what the measuring instruments are in any science which succeeds in taking us beyond the realm of speculation and personal opinion.

However, since the mind and personality are so complicated and variable, the use of tests by any but competently trained professional psychologists is comparable to a physician practicing without a medical degree. The popular use of tests in the schools by vocational counselors, who have had a few courses in psychology or maybe none, is dangerous. The self-styled psychologists who promise, with a battery of tests requiring only two or three hours, to outline a person's aptitudes and possible career, are far more audacious than legitimate psychologists who, after eight or ten hours of tests, may still be hesitant in their conclusions. Indeed, there are many situations in which the psychologist will decide that not one of the hundreds of tests available can be properly used. To give but one example, there are no valid psychological tests of journalistic aptitudes or writing ability. Writing, by its very nature, is originality in presenting ideas and events, poetry especially so. A psychological test is a *standardized* test, and a standardized test cannot measure originality, since originality means something that is not standardized.

Many people have asked me how they might become psychologists and there is a wide-spread confusion in respect to the kind of preparation required by the professional psychologist. A psychologist is a person who, after completing a college education, goes on to do graduate work in psychology leading to the degree of Ph.D. in psychology. The shortest time in which this degree can be obtained is by three years' full-time study at some recognized university giving degrees in psychology. It includes the preparation of a thesis based on an experimental study acceptable to the department of psychology. Psychologists who specialize in personal counseling, vocational guidance, business psychology, etc., must have additional training and experience in these fields. The basic courses in the preparation of a psychologist include, or should include:

Elementary and advanced experimental psychology in laboratory techniques
Statistical methods, elementary and advanced
Psychological tests and measurements, elementary and advanced
Social psychology
Abnormal psychology
Clinical and vocational psychology

One of the principal requirements for a college graduate who wishes to go on toward a Ph.D. in psychology is more than average training in mathematics. It is also desirable that the person should have had college courses in physics, chemistry and biology.

The official society for psychologists is the American Psychological Association founded in 1892. Most of the 2300 members of this association are teachers or re-

search workers in colleges and universities. Only in
recent years have psychologists begun to apply the results of their studies to the practical problems of individuals and institutions. The society for practicing psychologists, organized in 1937, and called the American
Association of Applied Psychologists, has about 400
members at the time of this writing. Psychologists have
been so backward and conservative in applying their
science, that much of their legitimate field has been pre-
empted by professions and people without adequate psychological training. These practitioners, with the bold-
ness of ignorance, have often made extravagant promises
in the name of psychology.

Psychology is not to be confused with psychiatry and
psychoanalysis. A psychologist is not a psychiatrist and,
by the same token, a psychiatrist is not a psychologist.
The psychiatrist is one who completes a regular medical
school course in which one-eighth or one-sixteenth,
sometimes none, of his courses are in psychology. He
may then serve as an interne in an insane asylum or in a
hospital clinic for mental cases in preparation for actual
practice.

Psychoanalysis is a set of doctrines and methods origi-
nated by Freud. Its most distinctive theories are that
dreams are the symbolic fulfillment of suppressed desires
and that many mental or emotional ills can be cured by
a prolonged series of talks probing the unconscious
mind. Psychoanalysis is accepted and practiced by many
psychiatrists but by very few psychologists. Both its
theories and its methods have been seriously questioned
by psychologists and more recently by certain psychia-

trists also. Psychology, in contrast with psychoanalysis, stands for a minimum of costly analysis and talk and a maximum of action and habit practice by the individual himself.

During the past sixty years especially, psychology has made great progress along scientific lines. Still a great deal of confusion and a great many false ideas and notions in regard to the field are current in the popular conception of psychology. This is only natural since even among professional psychologists, as here defined, widely different viewpoints still exist. My own interpretations of psychology will not be accepted by all psychologists today. Nevertheless they point, I hope, toward a greater degree of agreement among psychologists in the future and therefore also to a sounder understanding of psychology by the general public. For those who wish to go into this subject further, a short list of books and references is given in the Appendix.

III

THE PSYCHO-DYNAMICS OF
PERSONALITY

III

THE PSYCHO-DYNAMICS OF
PERSONALITY

A FAMOUS astronomer has announced his discovery
that the sun, among the stars, is a weakling and
gives off only seven-tenths of the warmth it should.
Fortunes have been given for telescopes by which to
gaze into the stars, but only trifles for telescopes by
which to study the personalities of men to discover the
secrets of their warmth. Colossal sums have been devoted
to the study of man's physical well-being, the diseases
which beset him and their cure. A bequest was recently
announced to create a foundation for the study of cancer. This one bequest alone, the sixth of its kind, represents probably as much as the total sum spent thus far by
all psychologists on specific studies of personality from
a psychological, not a psychiatric, point of view. Nevertheless, even these meager studies point to a disease of
personality, a veritable cancer of the mind, which
threatens, in my opinion, to decimate an entire civilization. All that has been gained in the control of man's
physical environment and well-being is being undone by
the failure to study in time his moral and spiritual well-

being. The situation is quite as though man had developed a universal blind-spot which enabled him to see everything but his true self.

The failure to study personality has been deliberately rationalized and defended as follows: Man is a mystery which defies solution. Unlike matter, which lends itself to scientific yard-sticks and the test-tube, the complications of human nature make such methods futile. We may scientifically measure certain aspects of the person, but the true person, the mystery of personality, forever eludes us.

It is said that the whole truth about anything, whether it be electricity or personality, will never be found by scientific methods. But if Benjamin Franklin had accepted this platitude with respect to lightning, our knowledge of electricity might be no further advanced today than is our understanding of personality.

It is not strange, in view of these circumstances, that personality has been so widely defined as a mysterious lightning, a divine spark, an intangible and indefinable something which certain people naturally have and others lack. Personality has also been described as a form of magnetism, a mysterious charm, a gift which some people only are fortunate enough to inherit. More recently it has been attributed to the glands, and medical men have claimed that the individual's personality, throughout life, is determined by his glandular structure. These notions, if true, present a very pessimistic view of the future to the individual and the human race.

Psychologists have found, however, that personality, far from being intangible, consists of definite habits and skills. These habits and skills can be acquired in the same way that people acquire the habits of writing and reading, that is, by practice and training. Almost every person, no matter what his heredity, can therefore improve or fail to improve his personality. Even people beyond middle age can create important changes in their personalities if they are willing to practice and to acquire new habits. Moreover, the basic habits and skills of personality can be measured, so as to give us a P.Q. or a personality quotient.

The P.Q. test and the many other tests of personality traits used by psychologists are, to be sure, crude measures of personality. They are no more capable of measuring the refinements, the higher developments of personality, than intelligence tests are capable of measuring the higher refinements of the mind. The I.Q. or intelligence quotient is a rough measure of the kinds of habits required to get good marks in school. It does not measure genius, although the term *genius* is often mistakenly applied to a high I.Q. The P.Q. or personality quotient is a rough measure of the kinds of habits required to get along in the world. The former is an index of what a person *knows* about things and people; the latter is a measure of what a person *does* about things and people. The two are relatively separate aspects of an individual's development, as indicated by the fact that a brilliant student is often a failure in practical life and a poor student is often a success once he gets out of school. This difference may be further illustrated by some examples not entirely foreign to common experience.

A young man of twenty-five, a college graduate, requested an examination which would reveal his aptitudes. For two years he had been working in the business department of a newspaper without making any progress. He had become convinced that he was in the wrong vocation, and that his future lay in finding a vocation for which he was by nature better adapted. A comprehensive series of tests indicated that his aptitudes fitted him for his present work as well as for any other. Tests of his personality traits and the facts of his history indicated that his basic problem was one of personality, a shortcoming which would handicap him in any vocation whatsoever. Therefore we recommended that he keep his present job, but that he undertake a program of social and physical activities which we outlined, activities which would lead to his development of a whole collection of new habits of dealing with people.

Just four years later he visited us again. "I came to tell you," he said, "that I have just received my fourth promotion. I am still with the same newspaper. My salary has almost trebled. I am satisfied that I am in the right vocation and am happy in my work." This incident is typical of many hundreds in our experience where the individual thought it necessary to find a vocation more suited to his aptitudes, but where the basic problem proved to be one of personality.

A salesman with a record of success asked us whether he had the capacities to study law and become a practicing lawyer. At the age of forty he was becoming tired of his work as a salesman; in fact, his productiveness had materially decreased. Our tests indicated that he possessed the necessary intellectual capacities for studying law. Nevertheless we advised him not to undertake the study of law for at least a year. "Your experience and the results of our personality tests," we advised him, "indicate the development of certain attitudes and habits which have definitely hurt your personality. Even if you pass the bar examinations, you would still have the problem of developing a practice. The defects in your personality would handicap you here even as they have already done in your selling. We suggest, for the next year, a program of activities which will renew some of your former habits and also add new habits to your personality. At the end of a year let us review the situation again."

When he returned a year later, the signs of his progress were clearly evident. He had carried out the program faithfully and with unexpectedly satisfying results. Even his productiveness as a salesman had increased so that his desire to study law could now be regarded as something more positive than an escape from the difficulties of his job. Although forty years old, he had been able to effect marked changes in his social habits in a very short time.

Both of these men were possessed of unusual intelligence and education. They had acquired many good intellectual habits and were ready to acquire more. What they needed to practice, however, were habits of a quite different kind. So clear cut is this difference between intellect and personality that practically all the available psychological tests reveal it with a high degree of consistency.

The tests devised by psychologists to measure aspects of personality now include the Thurstone Personality Schedule, the Allport A-S Reaction, the Root Extroversion-Introversion, the Bernreuter Personality Inventory, the Bell Adjustment Inventory, the Vineland Social Maturity Scale, the Link P.Q. or Personality Quotient, and many others. Most of these tests, some in many experiments, have demonstrated that there is little or no correlation between years of education or scholastic intelligence, and personality. That is, people with many years of education are almost as likely to rate low in these personality scales as are people with little education or low scholarship, and vice-versa.

On the other hand, all these personality tests give results which correlate highly among themselves. A person who rates high on one of them is likely to rate high on all, a person who rates low on one, low on all. That is, these personality scales measure approximately the same phenomenon, a set of habits quite different from the habits of the intellect as fostered by formal education.

The habits of personality thus isolated and measured, we find, are the habits which turn a person's energies outward into activities which interest and serve other people. They are the habits which give meat and substance to this intangible something called magnetism and charm. They are the habits which transform the divine spark, this mysterious lightning with which every person is endowed, into controlled and specific currents connecting him with other people.

Therefore I define personality as *the extent to which the individual has developed habits and skills which interest and serve other people.*[1] The individual must interest and serve others in making and holding friends, in getting and holding a job, in improving his position and salary, in starting and raising a family, in winning a place in the community. This definition of personality, as will become evident, embraces a range of habits far beyond that required to make social intercourse superficially easy. Its primary emphasis is not on conversational brilliance, or eloquence in public speaking, or on getting the better of people. Its emphasis is on doing things with and for other people. Its essence is self-sacrifice, not self-gratification. Indeed, the pursuit of personality just to win friends and position is quite likely to result in self-consciousness.

The process of converting undisciplined energies into the skills of personality consists not only of acquiring the appropriate habits but also of avoiding certain harmful habits. Probably one of the greatest of all hindrances in the development of personality is masturbation. I speak of it here because its importance as a factor in personality has been almost totally ignored, and does not

[1] This definition is consistent with that of many psychologists who define personality as the *social stimulus value* of a person. That is, personality is an *attribute*, a characteristic, like intelligence. A person has more or less intelligence, more or less personality. Some psychologists, however, define personality as anything which a person is. For example, G. W. Allport in his recent book, *Personality, a Psychological Interpretation,* gives this definition (p. 48): "Personality is the dynamic organization within the individual of those psychophysical systems that determine his unique adjustments to his environment." This is equivalent to saying that *personality is whatever a person is.* It makes *personality* synonymous with *person,* whereas our definition refers to certain qualities which one person develops and another fails to develop.

seem to be generally understood; also, because this problem goes to the very heart of the psycho-dynamics of personality. This practice takes some of the organic energies which are potential sources of charm, and disposes of them by a short-cut which has no reference to other people. In my work with young men, whether in respect to vocational, educational, or personality problems, I nearly always include a discussion of the psycho-dynamics of personality with some reference to masturbation, somewhat as follows:

"At birth the child is little more than an energy-creating organism. He eats and sleeps, and produces energy; but there is nothing he can do with these energies except wiggle and cry. He is like a dynamo with plenty of power, but not connected with any machines to transfer that power into useful action. Gradually, after much practice, the child acquires the habit of picking up and holding an object. One useful machine has now been attached to the power house. He acquires word-habits and a vocabulary, additional bits of habit mechanisms. He acquires the habits of crawling, of standing, of walking, running, jumping, all of which are mechanisms that further transform his energies into useful action. He learns to use his hands in writing, in eating, in throwing and catching a ball. The simpler habits later become the foundation of more complicated habit patterns, for example, tennis, where counting, running, catching, and talking are all important. Baseball, tag, music, swimming, dramatics, chores, Scout routines, etc., represent skills or habit mechanisms for expressing the energies smoothly in complex social situations.

"No one set of habit patterns is essential to a good personality, but a certain range of them is just as important in developing personality as are reading, writing, and arithmetic in developing the mind. And, since competitive games and social activities are usually voluntary, it is all the more important that the individual select certain ones and devote his energies toward their mastery. Whether he likes them or not at the outset is unimportant. As he acquires facility he may learn to like them, but the important point is that his energies are flowing outward in currents which will interest and serve other people. There is no charm in the energies except as these energies are skillfully expressed. And none of the skills of dealing with other people come naturally. They all require practice.

"The energies of sex are an additional source of potential charm, a magnetism which affects not only members of the opposite sex but members of the same sex also. Dancing is one of the habit patterns which directs these and the general energies in a manner which extends the range of one's social contacts among both sexes. Whatever the energy, its use in developing habits and skills of many kinds adds to the variety of people and situations in which we can be effective.

"We are told that the majority of young people practice masturbation more or less. Regardless of medical opinion that masturbation, within limits, has no injurious effects on health, its psychological effects may be very serious. It represents a short-cut, an easy method by which to express certain energies. Therefore it takes these energies out of the stream of slow, often tedious, practice by which the really useful skills are acquired. The body is like a river which dams up water so that it will turn machinery for useful work, but if the dam breaks, this stored-up power is wasted. Masturbation also encourages solitude and stimulating reading which still further keeps the person out of the group activities in which he should be spending his energies. In short, it may seriously interfere with the process of converting potential charm into actual charm.

"When this anti-social habit becomes a problem, the person usually tries to stop it by an act of will, but the will often fails and this is not the practical solution. The best solution is a more active participation in competitive games and group activities which take time and energy, and which substitute social interests for solitary interests. Gradually the threshold of resistance is thus raised, and the opportunities and skills for a normal expression of the energies are increased. Personality and charm are a result of the extent to which the individual has learned to convert his energies, his three meals a day and night's sleep, into habits and skills which interest and serve other people."

Our engineers and scientists have become masters of the dynamics of energy or power in machines. The techniques they have developed for utilizing the energies inherent in coal, water and electricity, and for eliminating friction and waste, are miracles of understanding and efficiency. With respect to the bodily energies, the most important of all forces, the physical and medical sciences leave us in comparative ignorance. The existing theories and practices in the medical, psychiatric field, too often emphasize the importance of rest and the dangers of fatigue. This emphasis tends to obscure rather than illuminate the basic facts about human energy. Fatigue or what seems like fatigue is often due to an excess of energies rather than to their exhaustion. The strenuous and skillful use of the energies automatically brings about genuine relaxation.

For example, a study of muscular relaxation among college athletes and college men who did not participate in athletics showed that the athletes relaxed more quickly and more completely after muscular exertion than did the non-athletes. In other words, those who systematically trained and used their muscles relaxed better than those whose muscles were little used. Relaxation comes from skilled exertion leading to a satisfying result. The tennis player who executes a fine stroke automatically relaxes for the next. The player whose strokes go poorly remains tense and is kept on the run by his more skillful opponent. Underlying the skill and relaxation of the superior player is the fact that, over a period of time, he has practiced two or three times as often and used up two or three times as much energy as has the unskillful player.

Not only in tennis but in conversation, in committee work, in church work, in teaching, in employment, dancing, bridge, and in all forms of social intercourse, relaxation, ease, come only as a by-product of strenuous practice. People often suffer from chronic exhaustion not because they are working too hard but because they have hoarded their energies in the past. Relaxation and emotional poise come from the lavish expenditure of one's energies, not from their conservation.

A clue to the psycho-dynamics of personality is revealed in the following incident: We examined a boy of nineteen who stuttered very badly and who had stuttered in all conversation since the age of twelve. This boy had run away from home and for two years had drifted around the country unable to hold a job. When asked to read aloud, he read a long and difficult paragraph without a single stutter. Physically his speech mechanism was quite perfect. His reading ability and intelligence were high. Upon going into his history we found that for two years he had played football on the high school team and, above all, had been the first string quarterback. "How could you play quarterback and give the signals when you stuttered so badly?" we asked. "Oh," he exclaimed, "I never stuttered when I played quarterback."

This episode reveals the secret of personality development. As a quarterback, if nowhere else, this boy had a good personality. Here was one situation in which he had applied his energies with determination and enthusiasm. He had practiced the plays and the signals until he knew them well. He had won the confidence of his team-mates and therefore more confidence in himself. He served his team with skill and forgot himself in this service. Here he did not stutter, and if he had achieved similar arts and skills in other social fields he would probably have stuttered less or not at all.

The ineffective personality, the unhappy person, is

usually one whose energies stutter, a person who stumbles through the social and economic relationships of life. There is a surplus of daily generated energies for which adequate habits of expression are lacking. Such a person is like an automobile with plenty of fuel, oil, and electricity, but a driver who is poor at shifting gears. There is plenty of power but the engine jerks, stutters, and stalls. The motor races and gears clash, but progress is slow. Other motorists blow their horns and the driver suffers anguish and chagrin. So in the case of every person moving in the traffic of life, there occur tensions and explosions, internal conflicts and frustrations, due to organic energies for which adequate skills of expression are lacking. Even the well developed personality stalls on occasion, but the poor personality grinds its gears and stalls continuously.

IV

THE HABITS OF PERSONALITY

IV.

THE HABITS OF PERSONALITY,

WHAT are the habits that convert a person's energies, his potential power, into smooth-flowing currents which interest and serve other people? The P.Q. or Personality Quotient test represents a definite step toward answering this question. In my work with people I had found that those who were happy or successful and who rated high in the already existing personality tests had usually developed certain habits which were lacking in unhappy and maladjusted people who rated low in these personality tests. There were many variations, of course, but with a wide range of case histories and with the advantage of previous personality tests I decided, about five years ago, to make a more scientific scale of these habits. That is to say, I planned to submit my personal experiences and conclusions to the experimental processes which characterize all scientific psychology.

My decision to construct this scale with reference to adolescents and high school children was based on the fact that they were old enough to have developed or failed to develop many of the basic habits and still young enough to be a reasonably homogeneous group. Moreover, this age seemed a good point from which to look both backward into childhood and forward into adulthood. From about five hundred habit items considered, two hundred were selected for a first experiment. These items were put into the form of questions somewhat as follows, each one representing a habit or an activity involving a whole collection of specific habits.

1. Games. Which of the following games and amusements do you engage in frequently in season? Indicate by a check mark ($\sqrt{}$) at the left.

Swimming	Track
Basketball	Bridge
Rowing or canoeing	Ping pong
Ice skating	Tag football
Tennis	Pool or billiards
Regular football	Roller skating
Boxing	Soft ball
Hockey	Riding
Catch baseball	Badminton
Regular baseball	Handball

2. Practice. Now go back over the above and put a check ($\sqrt{}$) at the right of those in which you practice hard and regularly so that you will become good enough to enter a contest.

3. Studies. Which of the following subjects do you like to study? Put an "L" opposite those you like to study and a "D" opposite those you don't like to study so well.

English   Geography
Arithmetic   Modern Languages
Algebra   Shopwork or Mechanical
History   Drawing
General Science   Physiology and Hygiene

4. Group Activities. In which of the following activities
   have you taken an active part for a year or more?
   Check (√) below.

> Boy Scouts
> Dramatics
> Sunday School
> School Society (Gen. Organization, etc.)
> Young People's Society or Church Club
> Glee Club or Choir
> Orchestra
> 4H Club
> Future Farmers of America
> Hiking Club

5. Hobbies. On which of the following hobbies do you
   spend or have you spent a great deal of effort or
   time? Check (√) at left.

> Stamp collecting
> Coin collecting
> Photography
> Machinery, mechanical work
> Playing a musical instrument
> Making and repairing radios
> Listening to the radio

Scrap book
Building models such as boats or airplanes
Collecting autographs
Collecting photographs
Nature study

The above questions are followed by a series of about one hundred fifty specific questions somewhat as follows:

How many summers have you spent at camp?
Do you keep a diary?
Have you learned how to do social dancing?
Do you have to do chores to earn your allowance?
Do you usually send birthday cards to the members of your family?
Have you served on any committees?
Do you sometimes sell magazines or tickets in order to raise money?
Do you like to introduce people to each other?
Do you often say: "I can't do this", or "I am no good at this"?
When you hear a good story do you usually tell it to others?

The answers to these and the remaining questions are entered by the persons being tested but these answers may be subject to confirmation by parents, teachers, or associates. There is a separate form for girls with suitable items and questions.

After three years of experimenting with the help of many psychologists and nearby high schools, the test was ready for a nation-wide experiment.[1] With the aid of eighty psychologists associated with the Psychological Service Center, it was tried out with eighty high school, junior high school and college freshman groups, according to a standardized program. From these results, nationwide standards were derived and the P.Q. formula developed. A P.Q. of 100 means that the person is average in his possession of the significant habits. P.Q.'s were found to vary from 50 to 140. A low P.Q. means that the person possesses a comparatively small number of the significant habits; a high P.Q. that he possesses comparatively many.

What are these significant skills and habits and how were they determined? The tests of several thousand subjects were taken and then divided into two groups, those whose P.Q. was above 100 and those whose P.Q. was below 100. Then each of the two hundred habit items was analyzed to discover which habits were most frequently possessed by those rating high in personality and which were most frequent or most often lacking in those who rated low in personality. This tremendous analysis required several months and the handling and

[1] Among the psychologists who supplied the major portion of the assistance in the earlier stages were Philip Corby, G. K. Bennett, Rose G. Anderson, Sydney Roslow, P. S. Achilles, and Dorothea Marston. The first report on the P.Q. test was published in the *Journal of Applied Psychology*, "A Test of Four Personality Traits," Henry C. Link, October 1936. The latest report embracing the findings of the nation-wide study may be found in the Manual of the P.Q. test, published by the Psychological Corporation, New York. The most complete independent study published thus far is: "An Evaluation of the P.Q. Test," William A. Thomson, Mooseheart Laboratory of Child Research and Carleton College, in the International Psychological Quarterly, CHARACTER AND PERSONALITY, June 1938.

computation of more than a million statistical items. It revealed that certain activities and habits were highly important, others moderately important, and still others of no significance one way or the other.

The group of activities and habits found to contribute most toward personality were the physical games and competitive sports. Casual participation was important, but systematic practice leading to participation in competitive athletic contests was still more important. This discovery of the part played by competitive athletics in developing personality is of major importance and will be discussed later.

Ping pong and bridge, among the social games, had a high value among boys and girls. Pool and billiards had a definite but lesser value for boys, checkers and chess a slight value. Social dancing was by far the most important of the social games, and in fact one of the most important of all the skills contributing to personality.

There is a tendency on the part of some people to say, in respect to statements like these: Lincoln had a great personality yet he did not play bridge; Florence Nightingale had a great personality yet she did not dance; there have been many great personalities who did not participate in athletic sports, etc. True, and our test shows that no one skill or habit is indispensable to personality or a high P.Q. In fact, any single habit pattern such as dancing, tennis, bridge, earning money, if practiced to excess, leads to a one-sided personality and may even result in the disintegration of character and personality. However, we are concerned at this stage not with personality in the rarefied atmosphere of the super-personality but with the *a b c*'s, the foundations of personality, the habits and skills which will enable most people to interest and serve others in the more common phases of living and getting along with people.

Frequently this question is asked: "How can the habits of personality be standardized or regimented without destroying individuality?" Just because all children must acquire the standard habits of the *three R's*, it does not follow that they cannot develop highly individual and specialized minds. Just so, the acquisition of certain basic habits of personality, the *four P's* in the P.Q. test, does not preclude the development of a distinctive personality. We have codified the basic habits of the mind through the grade schools, thus enabling people to communicate with each other through a common language. However, in the field of personality there is an almost complete vacuum at this point. We have not codified the basic habits of personality enabling all people to get along with each other and with themselves on a certain level. There lies the tragedy of our present civilization, namely in the extent of its intellectual habits and its failure to codify even the elementary habits of personality. There lies also the great hope for the future in filling this vacuum, toward which the present study and the studies of many other psychologists are now contributing.

To continue with the findings of the P.Q. study, dramatics and active participation in school societies, in the young people's society or church club, in the Boy and Girl Scouts, in Sunday School, all contribute toward personality. The test shows that activity in organizations like the Y.M.C.A. and glee club or choir contributes

more among boys than among girls, whereas member-
ship in an orchestra seems to be more important among
girls than among boys.

Playing a musical instrument, among the hobbies, contributes more in the case of girls than among boys. Coin
collecting is significant among boys and not among girls.
Photography, collecting photographs and autographs are
significant in both groups. Nature study was found to be
particularly important among girls, though also significant among boys. The hobby of listening to the radio
had no significant bearing, in fact was slightly negative,
among boys. Stamp collecting had a slight significance
for both sexes, and knitting for girls.

These results cannot be taken as an evaluation of these
respective hobbies, since our test does not distinguish between those who make much of a given hobby and those
who are more superficial. For example, playing a musical
instrument is one thing and playing it well enough to
entertain people or be in an orchestra is quite another
matter. More intensive experiments will undoubtedly
prove that the critical point is whether a hobby is merely
a matter of self-gratification or reaches the stage where
it will be a means of interesting and serving other people.
Thus far we can only say that the pursuit of hobbies as
such has some favorable effects on personality.

Doing well in scholastic studies was again found to
have little or no bearing on personality. The liking or
dislike for certain studies, however, was found very significant. The young people who liked most of their
studies, whether their marks were good or poor, tended
to have the better personalities, while those who disliked

their studies more frequently rated low in personality.

Arithmetic was the most significant of all the studies, especially among the boys. Here, as in studies of personality made by other psychologists, a liking for arithmetic was found to be highly characteristic of the more effective personalities. Arithmetic, of course, represents a set of habits which are of basic importance in dealing with other people fairly and squarely, not only in such simple acts as sharing the cost of a luncheon, but in keeping score, in the household budget, in business, in a thousand and one social situations.

So many people have asked: "Are these activities enumerated by your test the cause of personality or is personality the cause of these activities? Isn't it true that the good personality just naturally engages in social activities, while the poor personality just as naturally avoids them?" The answer is that no individual does anything naturally whether it be eating with a knife and fork or dealing with people. No matter what his capacities or tendencies by nature, habits and skills become natural only through strenuous and self-sacrificing effort. Just as the potentially good mind sometimes develops the habits of an actually good mind and sometimes just the opposite, so a potentially good personality may develop the habits of either a strong or a weak personality. This common question is just another way of stating the defeatist concept of personality which psychology now utterly repudiates.

"My daughter, age twenty," writes a mother, "had a wonderful personality and is beginning to lose it. My son, age eighteen, who lacked it completely, is beginning to develop a nice personality. I can see now just what happened. Our daughter was so smart with people that we allowed her to have her own way entirely too much. Her personality was too effective for her own good. She does pretty much as she pleases, has become selfish, and wangles her way out of many things she should do. Fortunately, we saw this in time to be firmer in our discipline of the boy. We insisted that he do the right things and now the results are beginning to show."

The child, in the beginning, has not the slightest concept of what to do, and learns only by the example and discipline of the parents. If the parents know what habits and skills are important, and then see to it that their children practice these skills, the children will be started in the right direction. The direction of a child's growth is infinitely more important than what a child actually is at a given moment. Only as the parents determine and discipline the child in the first place will the child later be able to determine and discipline himself.

All the habit items of the P.Q. test were evaluated with reference to four major groups of habits as well as with reference to the total result or P.Q. These four groups, called personality traits, were:

Habits of Self-Determination
Habits of Social Initiative
Habits of Economic Self-Determination
Habits of Adjustment to the Opposite Sex.

The trait self-determination, because of the habits it includes, gives us a remarkable insight into the development of personality. Among these habits the following are representative:

Persisting in games and sports even though awkward

Doing the less pleasant task first

Not using the words "I can't do this," or "I am no good at this"

The habit of controlling outbursts of temper

Finishing a task once started

Refusing to be discouraged

Not brooding over mistakes and hard luck

Having some definite vocational or educational plan.

Such habits represent the person who has been properly trained by his parents and who now says in effect: "There are certain things which I shall do whether they come easily or hard, whether I like them or not. I may be inferior in some of these things now but I do not have to remain inferior. I may be awkward and self-conscious in some of my attempts but I shall keep on trying nevertheless. I shall make mistakes and suffer for them, but I will not mope or remain discouraged. I will not be the victim of my environment or hard luck but will master it instead."

Such a person has set for himself certain standards and goals toward the achievement of which he subordinates pleasure and convenience. He is the exact opposite of the person who does only what he likes to do, when and as he likes, who avoids embarrassing or painful situations, who, instead of developing the habits of superiority, develops the habits of inferiority. Self-determination as contrasted with self-gratification, self-discipline as contrasted with self-indulgence, is the basic law in the development of personality.

The dynamics of acquiring skill in any field may be illustrated by the process of learning how to dive. The individual gets himself beautifully poised, leans forward, and at the last moment hesitates and draws back in fear. Again he makes the attempt and withdraws. With each hesitation and consideration his fears mount and his inclination to dive recedes. Finally, in angry desperation, he plunges in, arms and legs askew, and with a terrible flop. He comes up red and pained outside, chagrined and embarrassed inside. The comments and laughs of the spectators make him feel still worse. If, at this point, his fears prevent him from making further attempts, he may never learn to dive and his fear finally becomes insurmountable. He may rationalize this fear as a lack of interest in diving or, with typical inferiority of the times, he may vote for a movement to have the water made softer. If, however, he persists and continues to make awkward and painful dives, he will finally go in smoothly and come up feeling pleased. His friends will compliment his form and he will be on the way to one more conquest of himself and his environment.

Whether in diving or in any other phase of life, this is the basic psychology in the development of confidence and personality and there is no escape from this process. Again and again the individual must plunge into the stream of life, at this point and at that, in order to develop the skills which will express his energies smoothly and effectively in the company of other people, either in play or in work.

A young man once came to me with this strange request. "I wish," said he, "that you would tell me some things to do which I would dislike." Asked to explain himself, he related this experience. "I was engaged to a girl who liked to dance, play bridge, go to parties, watch athletic games, and be with people generally. I preferred going to lectures and concerts, attending open forums, or sitting with a few people discussing society and politics. She was not averse to such things occasionally, but I was not willing to learn bridge or dancing or to go to parties. I considered such pursuits frivolous and trivial as compared with the more intellectual pursuits. Finally she broke our engagement on the grounds that we had not enough interests in common.

"Just about then I read your statements to the effect that a person should undertake certain social activities which he disliked for the good they would do his personality. This and the breaking of my engagement led me to try. I joined a church club, learned to play basketball, played bridge, and became active in the affairs of the club. At first I was miserable, but as time went on I began to enjoy all the activities and sports which I had despised or feared before. In fact I liked them so well that I now want you to suggest something I will really dislike, because I want to keep on growing."

To do things merely because we dislike them is not a good reason, but to do them because they are desirable and because other people like them is the best possible reason. Many social activities may seem frivolous to us but not to others. Many of the requirements of a job may seem trivial to us but are important to our employer. The issue here is one of selfishness or unselfishness. Is the individual to be governed by the principle of what he likes, or what other people like; what he considers desirable or what others consider desirable? If he allows himself to be governed by the former and does always the things which will please him, his personality will shrink, his range of friendships will narrow, his likes will decrease while his fears and dislikes increase; whereas the person who acts on the principle of what will help or please others, even to the extent of undertaking activities which he dislikes or finds awkward, will develop new skills and in time even convert his aversions into enjoyment. The growth of a personality and the growth of a person's range of interests, skills and pleasures, are one and the same thing.

There is no danger of carrying this principle of pleasing and serving others too far except where a code of ethics or a standard of morals is lacking. It may be pointed out that the practice of serving others leads directly to a wider and wider range of skills and abilities. The employer, for example, nearly always rates higher on personality scales than do the rank and file of his employees, because he has learned so much better to help and serve other people. He serves not only his customers but his employees. In the professions, in the arts, and in every walk of life, this is true. Personality and its rewards are a by-product of converting one's energies into habits and skills which interest and serve other people.

At the opposite pole of personality as here described are the many people who eat heartily, sleep well, have had a fine education, converse well on certain subjects, especially themselves or the social order, write a good letter, have many ideas, have tried several jobs, are sure they could do well if they found something they liked but are now wretched with a sense of inferiority, distrustful of themselves, and therefore distrustful of others. Such people, young and old, frequently come for an examination to discover their aptitudes. Often our tests show that they have excellent minds, sometimes several aptitudes, but personality traits which rate somewhat as follows:

Habits of social initiative 17
Habits of self-determination 25
Habits of economic self-determination 13

Often they are people who have been subsidized by their parents or families which made it unnecessary for them to face the hard realities of life through which competence is developed.

In such situations we must sometimes say: "Your problem is not one of aptitudes or a vocation but one of altering your entire concept of life and your modes of living. Your present difficulty is due directly to the fact that you have always done as you pleased and have never been compelled to do certain things which, though difficult, would have been constructive. Instead of converting your energies in the service of others you have hoarded them for your own pleasures. Now these chaotic and inadequately expressed energies are tearing you to pieces." In such situations, depending on the case history, we must recommend a program of action far more comprehensive than the mere finding of a certain job, a program including a variety of activities such as described above. Where the individual undertakes such a program, the results are often remarkable.

The extremes of an undeveloped personality take such forms as delusions of persecution, suicidal tendencies, the fear of insanity, and a host of other paralyzing fears. The body may seem to be quite healthy but the person has lost the power to cope with himself or the world. The following case of a man who was beginning to suffer from a fear of crowds, even the fear of people to whom he was accustomed, is quite typical. He even dreaded his associates in the laboratory in which he worked as a chemist. Medical examinations could find nothing wrong with him. His physique was powerful, his appetite and digestion good, and he slept well.

Going into this man's history we found that his family had come to this country from Russia when he was twelve years old. They had slaved to advance his education and he had finally achieved a master's degree. He had then obtained a position as a chemist and for ten years had advanced at a reasonable rate. For eight years he had been married, happily so, although there were no children. The couple had lived a quiet, comfortable, and uneventful life. Now this unreasoning fear had come upon him and was growing in intensity.

We found that he had once belonged to a church, but in the pressure of getting an education had dropped out.

He had once practiced the violin with pleasure and devotion, but in five years had not touched it. He had for
some years worked as a dishwasher, a delivery boy, a
furnace tender, and in the summers as a road laborer,
but since gaining his position as a chemist, physical exertion had become almost unnecessary. He and his wife
lived in a convenient little apartment and with their
books and reading lamps were sufficient unto themselves.
Once struggling against great odds and absolutely dependent upon himself, he had achieved comfort and economic security. Now, in the midst of external security,
he had suddenly lost the security of his own soul. Once
ignorant in faith, he was now an educated man yet in
fear of losing his mind.

Here was a man with energies to burn in behalf of
his fellow men, whose excess energies were now burning him up instead. Here was a man who, because he
lacked children, friends, and committees to worry about,
was *forced* to worry about himself. Here was a man
who, in achieving his goal, had lost the power to enjoy it.

For every problem as serious as this there are hundreds
of thousands, representing various stages of personal
failure, unhappiness, and despair. In the majority of
these cases the difficulty is fundamentally the same, a
surplus of energies inadequately expressed, due to the
fact that the individual has been a law unto himself, and
has followed the selfish principle so widely expressed as
"living one's own life". There are, to be sure, break-
downs due to an unwise dissipation of the energies. Such
cases are rare in comparison with those resulting from a
selfish conservation of the energies. Unexpressed ener-

gies are bound to set up conflicts and frustrations, tensions and explosions. Their ultimate expression may take almost any form of abnormality.

There has been a great emphasis in recent years on the necessity for relaxation due to the growing tenseness of modern life. It has been said with great frequency that life is so fast and strenuous that systematic efforts for relaxation are becoming imperative. The psychodynamics of personality indicate that the exact opposite is true. Life in our civilization has become too slow to use up our energies. The automobile may be fast but we as a result move more slowly than before. The telephone is easier than the work of writing letters or calling on foot. Not long ago there was an advertisement saying: "Reach for the phone before you reach for your hat." The machinery is faster but we are more sluggish. Literally, our civilization is afflicted with a clogging of the organic energies.

Nation-wide studies of the use of leisure time, made by psychologists and other investigators, agree in their findings that by far the most popular leisure time pursuits are: listening to the radio, reading books and magazines, and going to the movies. The list of sedentary or spectator pursuits occupied far more time than did the pursuits requiring active participation.

Labor-saving devices have saved the energies of man, but to what end? To give him great leisure in which to stuff himself with the rich foods of excessive reading, excessive listening to the radio, excessive conversation and listening to speeches, an excess of all those pursuits in which he sits rather than moves, acts as a sponge rather than as a giver. These habits are common to young and old, rich and poor. They represent a retreat from life, adventure without fatigue, romance without risks, pleasure without pain, thinking without action.

Thus an entire nation constipates itself with the toxic substances of fear, distrust, inferiority, and despair. No wonder that crime, insanity, and class warfare have become so serious. The problem today is not one of improving a personality here and there but of elevating the personalities of an entire civilization.

The discovery that competitive athletic games make a major contribution to personality is consistent with the whole trend of modern civilization, representing as it does the over-emphasis on education and sedentary intellectual pursuits at the expense of physical activities. Indeed, nearly every one of the two hundred habits and activities which we have found contributing to personality involves the active use of the body and bodily energies. *So striking is this fact that we are compelled to regard bodily movement as the common denominator of personality, not any bodily activity, but those carried on with or in relation to other people in play or in work.*

Three hundred years of intensive science and education have produced the elaborate codification of the intellectual habits we so well know. Hundreds of courses in the grade schools, high schools, and colleges, each with its many textbooks, train students in these habits. Millions of manuals and books testify to the tremendous codification of the habits of the mind, but there is not yet a single textbook which codifies even the *a b c*'s of personality, and not one which is a required course in all the schools. The Bible, which comes closer to doing this than any other book, has not, on the whole, been interpreted by the church in terms of modern life. Toward such a codification scientific psychology has now made a beginning.

V

ON OVERCOMING FEARS
AND WORRIES

ON OVERCOMING FEARS
AND WORRIES

S OME years ago a Portuguese doctor, Egas Moniz, decided to operate on the brains of people suffering
from fears and worries. He deliberately destroyed large
segments of the brain tissue in the higher brain centers,
with successful results. Miraculous improvements in personality were effected. This operation, popularly known
as *psychic surgery*, constitutes one of the greatest discoveries in the history of man.

Following Dr. Moniz, a considerable number of American surgeons have developed this operation with brilliant
results. The brain tissue destroyed was always in the
frontal lobes of the brain, that is the higher brain centers,
the seat of reason and imagination. The nerve fibers or
mental pathways were cut in as many as twelve areas
each a half inch in diameter.

A woman, who had been confined to bed with day
and night nurses for a year, with extreme fears of all
kinds, soon after this operation was able to take care of
her own household, drive a car, and entertain people.
When she went to the theater, she was for the first time

able to enjoy the play and was not distracted by her distress over how her hair looked in back and other trifles of dress.

A bookkeeper of fifty-nine, bedridden for eight months, with a nervous breakdown, obsessed by a fear of poisoning, given to spells of weeping, and finally confined in a hospital with day and night nurses, after the operation lost all these symptoms. He had been in his old position as bookkeeper for several months when the case was reported. A man who had been a failure in business, after such an operation became a very successful salesman and later salesmanager. His wife reported that he made a much better husband after part of his brain had been removed. He did not find fault so much with details and stopped worrying about household affairs. He also developed a lack of self-consciousness and experienced no embarrassment if he made mistakes or received rebuffs. Tests of his intellectual processes, however, showed that these were of a continually lower order as evidenced by an increasing lack of discrimination.

Twenty-one such operations were reported in connection with the meeting of the American Medical Association last year. Most of them were immediately successful in wholly or partly eliminating such symptoms as excessive fears, worries, insomnia, delusions, crying spells, nervous indigestion, panic states, hysterical paralysis, etc. After destroying a good part of the higher brain centers, the lower brain centers, those which specialize in bodily action were given greater scope. The patients became at once more active physically. Usually there was also a slowing down of the higher thought processes, the reasoning powers, but patients considered this loss more than compensated for by a happier and more active life. The results of psychic surgery over a period of years are not yet known and many surgeons are still skeptical. Regardless of the final outcome, the present results are of major significance.

They are in perfect accord with the findings of psychologists that the intellect and imagination often become the chief enemies of personality; that thinking and analysis practiced at the expense of energy-consuming action are the great source of fears; that the lower brain centers, those which specialize in bodily action, are just as important as the higher centers of thought and at times even more important. Psychic surgery proves that certain people would be better off with less brains. It confirms what I have told so many people not yet in need of an operation, that *in their quest for happiness they should use their heads less and their feet more.*

A young man once told us that he suffered from the fear of not being able to go to sleep. Consequently he went to bed later and later but still could not sleep. He gave a long and technical description of how this state had come about. The real causes could have been stated in one sentence: too much thinking, reading, and talking, and not enough work and play with other people. "Can you help me to get rid of this obsession? Isn't there some process of relaxation you can teach me?" he asked. "None that will not do you more harm than good," we were compelled to tell him. "Then what can I do?" he implored. "Join a club or gymnasium," we advised, "and get into some regular competitive games." He objected on the grounds that this would take some time to arrange and he needed to do something at once. "Then run around the block at night until you are ready to drop," we recommended. "You do not need relaxation, you need exertion. You have put too much of your physical energy into thinking and imagining things. If you run around the block, you will have to use some of these energies through your lower brain centers, the part that drives the body and the legs. If you run hard enough and often enough, you will automatically relax. You have thought yourself into this fear with your mind; you can run yourself out of it with your legs." And he did, and found sleep without the use of sedatives.

On one occasion we gave similar advice to a man obsessed by the thought of committing suicide. He, also, was the product of too much thinking and imagination, with too little practice in the habits of action. He, too, objected to the delay in undertaking the program of activities we suggested. "Then run around the block until you drop dead," we advised him. "If you are going to commit suicide anyway, you might at least do it in a heroic fashion." He tried it, not once but several times, and each time he felt better—in his mind if not in his muscles. Finally he joined an athletic club and began to participate in competitive sports. He was then well on the way to a more normal frame of mind and to a better command of his job, which was largely sedentary and intellectual.

A life on the running track or in the gymnasium is by no means the complete solution for all worries; but when an individual has churned his thought centers into a turmoil, the sharp diversion of his energies into bodily action is often a first step in achieving a better balance. The individual himself, instead of the surgeon, reduces the over-activeness of the mind.

Fears do not just happen. They are developed by practice just as we perfect all other habits, good and bad. We nurse and feed them until, from inconsequential trifles, they sometimes grow to monstrous proportions. The reasoning by which Dr. Moniz arrived at psychic surgery is stated by him somewhat as follows: "While there are no visible abnormalities of the brain in certain mental disorders, the symptoms might be due to the development of certain habits in the higher brain centers which act toward the detriment of personality as a whole. By forcibly breaking up the connections or nerve fibers on which these bad habits have been developed, these habits are eliminated and the person is given the opportunity to build up new habits along different lines."

What new habits? And along what new lines? And why were the proper habits not built up in the first place so that the practice of fifty years need not be curtailed by a few minutes of psychic surgery? This is the problem with which psychology, as distinguished from psychiatry and medicine, is concerned. This is the field in which psychology is rapidly filling the gap left by the other sciences.

I am reminded of a woman sixty years old who for many years had been subject to severe fits of depression lasting several weeks at a time. For over thirty years she had worked in the same bank. She lived with an older sister who was partly dependent on her. When these spells of depression came she was made totally unfit for her duties, but her employers had been very lenient about her absences. Her case had originally been diagnosed as manic-depression with very little hope for the future. Other psychiatrists, whom she consulted later, not only in her home town but elsewhere, had advised: "When you feel one of these spells coming on, drop everything and have a change of scene. Take a boat trip or a trip to New York. See the shows and the sights. Get out of your rut and keep going until you feel better."

She had done this now for several years, at the expense of her savings yet with some relief. Again she was in New York on one of these trips. "But," she told us, "the effects have been growing less. I have been traveling for ten days now, going to plays, concerts, and lectures, taking in the sights, but it isn't doing me any good. I am in the depths of depression. I have gotten out of my rut but my trouble still follows me. I have run away from home, *but I can't seem to get away from myself!*"

Our inquiries showed that she was a woman of unusual background and culture, but one who had lived a highly self-centered life. About the employees in the bank, with many of whom she had worked for years, she knew almost nothing. Satisfied with a few friends, she had made little effort to cultivate new ones. A strong woman, physically, with excellent appetite and a good health record, her life was essentially sedentary—at work, at home, and even in her diversions.

We advised her, among other things, to ask the names of the tradesmen who served her, to inquire about their work, their hours, their families. When last heard from, she had become so involved in visiting and helping the families of two of these people that her letter was entirely about them with little reference to herself. Having become absorbed in their troubles, she had less energy left for her own. Having tried for years to buy happiness, she was finding it more effective as well as cheaper to give happiness. In the process she had begun to acquire a new set of habits, habits conducive to self-forgetfulness and happiness.

A mother of six children gave this significant summary of her life: "As a young woman I was troubled with many fears, one of which was the fear of insanity. After my marriage and the birth of our first child, these fears still persisted. However, we soon had another child and ended up by having six. We never had much money and I had to do all my own work with practically no help. Whenever I started to worry about myself, the baby would cry and I would have to run and look after him. Or the children would quarrel and I would have to straighten them out. Or I would suddenly remember that it was time to start dinner, or that I must run out and take in the wash before it rained, or that the ironing had to be done. My fears were being continually interrupted by worries about my family, most of which were fears into which I had to put my back. Gradually my fears about myself disappeared, and now I look back on them with amusement."

The moral of this episode may not be to have six children, but it is incontrovertibly true that the smaller families and increased leisure of our time are conducive to the generation of fears and warped personalities. People who enjoy this leisure can overcome its dangerous possibilities only by voluntarily involving themselves in community activities which will add to their worries *about other people;* which will necessitate the use of their energies more fully in behalf of other people. I used to smile, with the intellectual cynicism common to our age, at the ladies' auxiliary gossiping over their sewing for charity. Now I pay them tribute. In fact, if the condition of admission to all forums discussing the affairs of the world were sewing and knitting, by the men as well as the women, we would probably have fewer forums and those remaining would produce a more useful result.

During one of my vacations I observed an elderly Englishman doing needlepoint. Whether sitting alone or chatting with other people he was usually busy with his design. One day I ventured to ask him the reason. His reply was that he had a tendency to brood when alone and to talk too much when in company, and had found this hobby a convenient and effective antidote to both faults. Actually, if people worried more over their knitting, they would have fewer worries and fears about themselves. This is not an attempt to be facetious. The better institutions for mental cases are increasingly substituting handicrafts and work for analysis and talk as sound therapeutics for nervous ailments. Knitting or activities requiring the use of hands and body, if adopted now, may make them less necessary later. And if these activities require coöperation with other people, their value is infinitely greater.

Sometimes, to be sure, people who have lived an extremely active life also acquire fears. I remember a man of thirty-six who had engaged in many of the activities that have here been described as desirable. Yet, though happily married, he was miserable, depressed, and afraid of the future. A more careful study of his history revealed the fact that his life had been one of rebellion against all the ideals and convictions of his father who was a minister. Disregarding the teachings of his father, he did as he pleased. But, although he took up many activities, he followed them only so long as they gave him satisfaction. Aided by his education, he was able to justify and to rationalize his own desires and to dispose of the restraints imposed by religion and its moral codes when they interfered with his pleasures.

Now, although he made a good appearance, talked well, and had what seemed like a pleasant personality, his mind was in a turmoil. The more he thought and planned the more confused and fearful he became. He had destroyed all religious and moral certainties in his life. He was like a train running without a track, full of power but with no sense of direction.

One of the chief causes of unnecessary and wasteful thinking is the absence of mental tracks, that is a moral code, a religion, or a set of fixed principles. The person who takes certain standards of right and wrong for granted does not have to waste his energies in thinking about them. They serve as a track for his energies. Instead of dissipating his reason on ripping up the old tracks and thinking out new tracks, he is free to devote his energies to the process of getting somewhere.

The statement has often been made in recent years that the whole world seems to have lost its mind. I should say rather that the world had lost its standards and morals. Therefore, like the man just described, its mind is in a turmoil. Individuals and nations are all trying to lay their own tracks. Each strives to create a new social or personal order.

Indeed, the intellectual fad of the times is to deprecate ancient moral truths because "we are living in a rapidly changing social order in which the old must be judged by the new." The popular contempt for ancient truths and moral standards inevitably creates internal conflict in the individual, collisions between groups and nations, general uncertainty and mounting fears. There are some beliefs in life that are higher and more important than the higher thought processes and that release the energies for harmonious action.

At the bottom of most fears, both mild and severe, will be found an overactive mind due to an underactive body; too much energy churning the higher brain centers in vicious circles, not enough energy driving the arms and legs and hands in useful work or play. Even soldiers going into battle become less afraid in action than they were in the suspense of waiting for the signal to attack. We have described the act of learning to dive, and the experience of the young man learning to do the things he disliked, and the woman who learned to forget herself in the service of others. Such instances illustrate the basic psychology of overcoming or avoiding fears in every phase of life. Even children, whose fears were initiated by the mistakes of their parents or by some unfortunate experience, can overcome their difficulties only by a program which substitutes action for introspection. People generate fears while they sit and overcome them while they move.

Before me as I write is a letter from a young woman beginning: "Ever since I was sixteen years old I have been afraid to start a conversation." The letter goes on to enumerate other fears including a fear of her employer, the fear of losing her job, a fear of men, fear of driving a car, a fear of confiding in friends, the fear of reading a report at the girls' club, and several others to the total of eleven. All of them were fears on the level of common human experience. Except for details, this letter is like hundreds of others, and some of its experiences are probably common to millions of people. In almost every case, the net result of these fears is the same, a sort of creeping paralysis, a feeling of misery, of suffocation, of panic, of defeat.

Many fears are literally cultivated by too much reading, thinking, and talking. They may begin with some one experience or shock, but usually with an apparently innocent habit. In either case, whole networks of habits conducive to fears are often developed by excessive reading, listening to the radio, self-analysis or the analysis of others, and a host of other easy and pleasant pursuits.

The young woman who spends all her spare time reading fervent love stories tends to become increasingly afraid of actual men. The person who habitually analyzes and questions the motives of his friends becomes increasingly afraid of people. Employees often analyze the acts of their employers to an extent which hastens the day when fear will make them incompetent employees. Children learn to argue with masterful logic against what their parents wish them to do, thereby practicing the very habits which will make them afraid to do these things when later they see them desirable. The mother who avidly reads the voluminous literature on bringing up children becomes increasingly fearful of how to discipline them. The person who studies and talks about all his physical symptoms may end up as a chronic hypochondriac. The individual who becomes absorbed in the literature of self-improvement too often acquires a whole collection of mental hazards. From such habits of intellectual self-gratification, substituted for a strenuous and sometimes painful program of action, grow many of the more devastating fears.

So many young people complain about their fear of conversing and being friendly with strangers or slight acquaintances. They become paralyzed in company, do not know what to say, and are afraid to say anything because it might prove embarrassing. Yet such people can often write ten-page letters analyzing their difficulties with great intelligence and logic. They often have excellent minds, are experts at sizing up other people's faults, and love a good argument. They are often the young people who, when mother says: "Susan, I wish you would take Towser out for a walk," reply: "Oh, mother, I just must finish this story." Or, when mother says: "Frank, will you run down to the grocer's for a quart of milk?" say: "Mother, I simply must hear the end of this program."

The simple act of taking the dog for a walk is one of the most fruitful sources of friendly acquaintances. People smile and speak to us simply because of our dog. I never did get acquainted with one of my neighbors until our dogs got into a fight. Mine wore a muzzle and his did not. His dog finally got my dog by the leg and held him squealing; but after I had given the neighbor's dog a vigorous kick, choked his collar, and twisted his tail until he opened his jaws, all in the presence of his owners, we became quite friendly neighbors. The dogs, the feet and the hands did in five minutes what six months of living near each other had failed to accomplish.

To many people, afraid to converse with others, we have recommended such games as ping-pong, and especially bridge. "While playing bridge," we have told them, "you do not need to be a brilliant or a steady conversationalist. In fact, you may be all the more welcome because you do not talk so much, but keep your mind on the game and listen to what has been bid. Not being under the pressure to make conversation, you will find it easier to put in an occasional remark."

Strenuous games break down the barriers between people even more quickly than do the milder pursuits. Everybody knows that a group of people playing any active group sport soon get to shouting. Under such physical exertion they will be shouting to a teammate, a stranger till that day, and calling him by nickname. In one session of strenuous physical effort more progress in friendship is made than in a year's carefully planned conversation. Any individual with social fears might become this stranger. It is inconceivable that the Y.M.C.A.'s, the Y.W.C.A.'s, and similar organizations are not treble in number and overwhelmed with members. In such places and not in books or in lectures lies the remedy for many fears.

The more general fears, such as the fear of insanity, of persecution, of inferiority, of crowds, are usually the result of a failure to conquer enough of the minor fears by practicing the right habits. Sometimes, however, they are due to some shocking experience such as the loss of a job, financial reverses, disappointment in love, or the death of a dear relative. Such an experience often leads a person to withdraw from life, to develop habits of retrospection and distrust of the future and himself.

A man of fifty-six, who had been with one company for thirty years, after losing his position began to mope and to withdraw from all contacts not only with his family but with his former friends and acquaintances. Within six months he had become a bundle of fears, an almost helpless individual. Finally he was persuaded to visit a distant relative who owned a farm. Without realizing it, he was drawn into the physical routines of the establishment. In six months he was himself again.

A mother suddenly lost her only child, a daughter of fifteen. For a year she grieved and grew increasingly melancholy. The husband had his business to keep him going in the right habits. Finally the mother adopted two babies. Now she worries on her feet instead of in an easy chair. Her energies, instead of piling up and creating tensions, as happens when the frontal lobes get in the way of the centers of action, now chase her about in bursts of happiness or irritation. She has built up habits which consume bodily energy instead of habits which compel this same energy to consume the mind. Her worries are ones she would rather keep than have removed. She still thinks of her lost child, but these images are a treasured memory rather than a monstrous master.

Millions of people on relief and part-time W.P.A. work are sitting around cultivating fears. They are not very different from millions of children subsidized by their parents to live a life of ease and irresponsibility. Both groups may be improving their minds at the cost of increasing their fears. The most comprehensive answer is a more strenuous life of physical exertion in company with other people. Unless our educational system, for adults as well as for children, changes its emphasis, we may yet have to put one-half our population into C.C.C. camps in order to cure the fears which trouble a nation.

Far better than drastic social compulsions are the decisions which the individual makes for himself and the habits he cultivates as a free and responsible person. His parents and environments may be responsible for him in the beginning but only he can be responsible for himself in the end. The brilliant success of psychic surgery emphasizes this fact. Psychic surgery is a mechanistic, an external approach to the problem of personality. It may give relief and it may even give happiness, but by a step which leaves a man or a woman less of a human being; by destroying in man the very elements which make the highest achievement of intellect and personality possible. It says, in effect: "If you cannot properly use the gift

of a perfect human brain, you are better off without it."
The basic problem, therefore, is a psychological one
rather than a medical or a neurological one, a problem
of developing personality from within by the individual
himself rather than of having it remade from without.

Fears and an ineffective personality go hand in hand.
The person with fears is one who has failed to convert
enough of his energies into habits which interest and
serve other people, both in play and in work. Fear is
nature's warning signal to get busy. In its mild and initial
states it takes the form of chronic dislike or criticism of
people and activities.

Just as fear paralyzes the body, so rage energizes it.
Psychologists find that normal people have more bursts
of energy and excited activity than do subnormal people. Anger is psychologically closely related to fear. A
little push will often transform fear into anger, and
anger primes the body for a constructive decision and a
program of fear-destroying action.

In the foregoing very little has been said about the
great power of religion in overcoming fear. Insofar as
religion remains, as it so often does today, a sedentary
pursuit confined to sitting in church on Sundays, it falls
far short in helping to overcome fears. A religion, which
does not influence people to do during the week what
they would otherwise not have done, is a religion merely
of the higher thought centers.

I have heard so many people say of sermons they have
just heard: "What a powerful sermon that was! Rev-
erend Blank certainly put his finger on what's wrong

with the world. I agree with everything he said." When I sometimes ask such people: "Did anything he said make you want to do something right away, or do differently something you are now doing? Did his sermon make you feel uncomfortable or dissatisfied with yourself?" the answer is usually a stare of bewilderment.

My concept of religion and a religious sermon is something that will make me feel ashamed of myself, something that will stir me to action, something that will compel me to do things for other people at the expense of my private pleasures and comfort. A reading of the New Testament will show that nearly all of Christ's sermons and conversations fulfilled these conditions. He was not a popular preacher. When the multitude followed him hoping for a new kingdom and an easy abundant life, he preached his great sermon: "Beware of covetousness: for a man's life consisteth not in the abundance of the things which he possesseth." Nevertheless he made his disciples work to give the multitude relief from hunger. He preached a life of action and he lived as he preached. He conquered all fears, even the fear of death.

Religion, in many instances, has become too much an exercise of the higher thought centers at the expense of energy-consuming action with and for other people. But religion as exemplified by its great exponents is a source of power. It can give the individual a faith in the universe and in himself that will move mountains. The great religions have insisted on this truth, which psychology now scientifically confirms, that the individual is not the victim of a heartless environment but a creature of infinite possibilities. This conviction and the power which it gives is the final solution to the individual's conquest of himself, his environment, and his fears.

VI

MACHINISTS OF THE SOUL

MACHINISTS OF THE SOUL

A PSYCHIATRIST in charge of a so-called *soul clinic* announced some years ago * a cure for chronic alcoholism through the withdrawal of spinal fluid and the consequent reduction of a high brain pressure. In some people, he states, alcohol leads to increased intercranial pressure, which in turn leads to emotional instability and a further craving for alcohol. Through the withdrawal of spinal fluid and certain other medical steps, this pressure is brought down to normal, whereupon the individual permanently loses his desire for alcohol. Moreover, he claims that "an exquisite refinement of judgment takes place of the grosser qualities, so that as the patient goes on in life you are particularly struck with the extraordinarily fine quality of mental and emotional balance. The petty reactions to irritation disappear, the personality is integrated and stabilized, the moral nature is completely regenerated."

That any physical cure will lead to "extraordinarily fine qualities of mental and emotional balance" and to

* "A New Pathology and Treatment of Chronic Alcoholism," Edward Spencer Cowles, M.D. *Medical Journal and Record*, May 20, 1931.

"an integrated and stabilized personality," unless the individual possessed them before his alcoholism began, is more than doubtful. That this particular cure will even remove the fundamental causes for drinking is open to serious question.

Among a considerable number of chronic or intermittent alcoholics, who have come under my academic observation, the majority presented a history in which alcoholism was clearly an escape from the painful realities of living. Their troubles usually came first, the resort to alcohol came later. Either an unfortunate marriage, or financial difficulties, or the inability to cope with life generally, created a desire for escape which alcohol was found to provide. If their desire for drink was artificially cured, the conditions that led them to drink in the first place would still remain. Such people suffer from a pressure far more important and comprehensive than the pressure of an intercranial fluid. The latter, when all the facts are known, may be found a physical incident due to many causes other than the use of alcohol. Alcohol, not unlike masturbation, is often a short-cut to release from pressure and tension. Since the energies cannot be expended in normal dealings with people, they are side-tracked through such a device.

The ineffective or maladjusted personality generally is one whose energies seem to be blocked in their expression. Individuals themselves usually realize this fact and describe its manifestations in definite symptoms. "I am in a continual state of mental unrest, constantly driven by a desperate, relentless urge, seeking for a means of escape, and at times overwhelmed by a sense of futility and defeat." "My mind is racing ninety miles an hour and my body is stalled. When I am with other people I know I should say or do something, but I hold back, I grow rigid, I clench my hands, I even break into a sweat." "I have an excess of energies for which there seems to be no outlet. Life seems to hem me in." Statements of this sort could be quoted indefinitely. In more or less extreme form, they apply to most cases of undeveloped personality.

Therefore, since the energies have a definite physical basis, it seems only logical to suppose that most maladjusted personalities within the normal range should show some pathological sign of physical tension or pressure, and quite likely a sign, which, like intercranial pressure, affects the higher brain centers in a comprehensive fashion. Such a discovery, which is not at all unlikely, would constitute an interesting confirmation of the psychological concept of the psycho-dynamics of personality.*

* Since this chapter was written, some remarkable discoveries of just this kind have been announced. Insulin has been successfully used in treating schizophrenia and mild epilepsy. Schizophrenia is the name given to mental disturbances in which the more common symptoms are great nervous tension, irritability, intense fear, delusions of persecution, etc. Dr. E. G. Hall and Sir Frederick Banting of Toronto attributed their cures of schizophrenia to the action of insulin in causing a great rush of blood away from the brain and a subsequent lowering of the blood supply to one-fourth of normal. In Dr. Hall's words, a "cerebral anemia" or starvation of the brain was produced and this treatment resulted in remarkable cures of schizophrenia.

Another group of physicians in Boston has found insulin not only helpful in treating schizophrenics but in obtaining remissions of seizures by mild epileptics. Dr. W. G. Lennox, reporting these studies, also points out that schizophrenia, epilepsy, and many other psychopathic states, manifest the same kinds of brain waves. Therefore, he

At the present time, this psychological concept is very much obscured by the tendency of so many psychiatrists to attribute personality problems to exhaustion or fatigue instead of to bad habits. "Most psychoneuroses are caused by fatigue," says one of the country's best known psychiatrists. "Suppose the normal nerve energy to be one hundred. In healthy persons this runs down at times to eighty, owing to the wear and tear of daily living. Normally, this loss is repaired by sleep, rest, relaxation, diversion. But let the supply of energy drop below eighty to sixty, and the patient is in a neurasthenic state. In this state he is acutely conscious of his sensory system, of how he feels. He is subject to headaches, to fears, to indigestion. Painful memories dating from childhood well up into his consciousness and become magnified into fear complexes. He loses his sense of security. Physiologically, sociologically, psychologically, he is in a state of fear." The psychiatrist's treatment for such conditions

---

believes that these different mental ills may be forms of one basic trouble.

Such findings certainly confirm our psychological analysis that many fears, worries, and serious mental ailments are due to a clogging of the energies, to what might be called "cerebral indigestion." Too *little* energy is used up in bodily activities, too *much* energy goes to the higher brain centers. Insulin shock and artificially produced "cerebral anemia" may effect at least temporary cures, but we are still far from the real causes of these ailments. A better clue to these causes may be psychic surgery, which destroys large sections of the brain completely. With fewer brain tracts, especially in the cortex, less energy is called for use in mental processes. There is a more permanent cerebral anemia, so to speak.

Thus our concept of the psycho-dynamics of personality seems to receive important supporting evidence from the field of medicine. The essence of this concept is that the maladjusted personality is one suffering from a surplus of energies due to the lack of a proper range of habits and skills by which to express these energies smoothly.

is essentially one of rest and relaxation, frequently including the use of bromides, coupled with suggestions to calm the patient's fears.

This theory and treatment are perfectly calculated to attract those people who have habitually sought an easy escape from life and its personal responsibilities and who are only too glad to believe in a pleasant remedy for their present state. The wear and tear of modern living is one of the popular pseudo-scientific fictions which people, anxious to shift their responsibility to others, are only too willing to believe.

No doubt some people are exhausted by an unwise or extravagant use of their energies. However, in our experience personality problems have usually arisen from too much rest, from the lack of energy-consuming activity. Instead of being exhausted by the wear and tear of modern living, they are exhausted by a life of ease, by procrastination, by dodging their responsibilities, by the constant choice of the easy path instead of the right path. Therefore they suffer from an excess of accumulated energies and from consequent tensions and worries which often lead to an artificial fatigue. They are, so to speak, poisoned by their own energies. What psychiatrists now so often regard as exhaustion, the psychologist would describe as a *clogging of the energies*. The treatment for permanent results is not rest but a program of energy-consuming action, not artificially induced sleep but the sleep of genuine physical exhaustion. It consists not of what a doctor can do for the individual but of what the individual can be induced to do for himself.

Another mechanistic or external approach to personality problems is that represented by endocrinology. Some years ago we gave a vocational examination to a young man of twenty at the request of the endocrinologist who had been treating him. Our examination revealed that the problem was one of personality, the failure to have achieved basic habits and skills in common social adjustments. The glandular treatment, as a matter of fact, had been instituted as a means of restoring physical and emotional balance in this young man. Now, when we suggested a plan for a vocation to which he was intellectually suited, he continued to fall back on the need for a more adequate *balance* through further treatment. He had become expert in the vocabulary of endocrinology and every practical step we suggested was postponed because he was either overbalanced or underbalanced at the moment. He had become definitely a hypochondriac. The endocrinologist may have achieved a physical cure, but in the process had made the young man dependent on medicine and on him.

The *glands regulating personality* is a concept of increasing importance in the medical field. The thyroid, a famous surgeon announced, produces a hormone which determines whether a person is a dullard or genius. By stimulating this gland in certain ways higher and better mental achievement can be brought about. The dullard and genius represent extremes of glandular activity. "So many individuals of Phi Beta Kappa rank are to be found among patients of hyperthyroidism that in a certain sense we may say that Phi Beta Kappa itself is a disease." If this is true in the sense that the doctor meant it, parents may soon hope to solve their children's school problems by a note to the physician: "Please stimulate Mary from an average of 50 to an average of 80 or better."

Inferiority complexes may be overcome in the near future, and backward, retiring individuals developed into geniuses, announces another endocrinologist, by the use of the hormones from the pituitary gland. In this case it is to be done by stimulating the bodily growth of a possible short person to that of a six-footer. Since the inferiority of many capable individuals is due to their short stature, he claims, the removal of this handicap will tend to give them superiority. Thus, even the sense of inferiority in men who are too short and in women who are too tall is to be cured by glandular treatment rather than by what such individuals can do for themselves.

Thus do the machinists of personality approach this group of problems.

A prize example is that reported in a great newspaper under this title: "Why is a Sot? Science Knows: He is Allergic to Alcohol." The article describes a report to the American Psychiatric Association by Dr. Robert V. Seliger of Johns Hopkins University, 'Like the hay fever sufferer who becomes oversensitive to pollen, many drinkers get allergic to alcohol. This allergic effect, according to Dr. Seliger, explained many cases of habitual intoxication. The person is really sick. When appealed to on moral grounds, this sort of alcoholic allergic takes refuge in drinking still more. But if he understands that he is suffering from an allergy, the drinker is more likely

to treat himself as he would in any other form of disease.'
In short, he will pay a doctor to accept the responsibility
for his alcoholism!

The illustrations given could be multiplied indefinitely
and might even include such extremes as face-lifting and
the use of monkey glands to restore the energies of
youth. Whatever the merits of these many medical devices, they all represent attempts to construct or recon-
struct personality by external means rather than through
the efforts of the individual himself. They transfer the
problem of personality from the individual to his psychiatrist, his neurologist, his endocrinologist. If we follow this trend to its logical conclusion, we arrive at a
race of medical guinea pigs, or a collection of puppets
which, in place of souls and will-power, have physicians
to move them.

We have been discussing the definitely medical ap-
proaches to personality. However, it is in the less obviously medical field that psychiatry and psychoanalysis
go farthest in destroying the foundations of character
and personality. Here we find a collection of speculative
and pseudo-scientific theories which have already helped
to undermine the morals and thinking of a civilization.
Moreover, many of these theories and the therapy they
lead to are absolutely contrary to the facts of psychology.

Psychiatry, as a branch of medicine, has developed a
classical body of observations and treatments in the field
of insanity and extreme abnormality. This body of
knowledge rests almost wholly on institutional cases or
cases bordering on the institutional. However, in recent

years psychiatrists have tended to extend their activities into the whole field of mental hygiene and the more normal problems of personality, and have done this without any adequate disciplines or knowledge to prepare them for this responsibility. Their theories and practices in this field are extremely chaotic, and no professional standards comparable to the standards in the orthodox medical field have been developed.

Moreover, instead of turning to the profession of psychology for scientific facts in respect to the emotions and habit formation, psychiatrists have too often swallowed the speculative and unscientific theories of psychoanalysis. These theories, with their over-emphasis on sex, prolonged analysis, dreams, and the sub-conscious, have been widely practiced. Indeed some of the more conservative leaders in the psychiatric field have formally warned their colleagues against their credulous acceptance of psychoanalytic doctrines.

As an example of the psychoanalytic influence in psychiatry, the following quotation is illuminating: "The characteristics of all habits," says one of England's leading psychiatrists, "is that they are spontaneous and spring from unconscious motives. Bad habits, such as a bad temper, perversions, a habit of contradicting, or self-depreciation, are due to repressed morbid complexes. Behind every habit is an emotion, the arousal of which determines habit. The arousal of certain repressed emotions gives rise to the habit. If the complex is eradicated the habit ceases immediately as the electric light when the current is turned off. It may take weeks and months to discover the complex, but when discovered the habit or phobia which sprang from it is immediately eradicated." Here are six statements which express ideas widely accepted by psychiatrists and psychoanalysts yet all of them are contrary to the principles of habit formation we have already described.

Habits are not spontaneous but are acquired and fixed by practice and repetition. Bad habits are not the results of repressed morbid complexes; rather, the complexes are due to the bad habits. The emotion does not determine the habit; rather, as pointed out before, the habit determines the emotion. If the complex is found and eradicated the bad habit does not automatically disappear. Occasionally, yes, but often it persists as strongly as ever.

The statements quoted are not only psychologically false; they are exactly the kind of doctrine which leads people to believe that they are not responsible for their bad habits; which encourages them to believe that they can get rid of their bad habits through prolonged talks with a practitioner; and which puts the practitioner at the very outset in an impossible position. *He* has now assumed the responsibility for the person's bad habits and he, not his patient, is going to eliminate them. This is undermining personality with a vengeance. This is a doctrine wholly contrary to the doctrine of free will and individual responsibility.

A well grown boy of seventeen once came to us and, within a few minutes, blurted out the difficulty we had already suspected. "I will tell you quickly what my problem is," he began, "because I have talked and been talked to so much about it that I can't stand talking

about it much more. It is masturbation. I have been psy-
choanalyzed and when that did no good I had a series
of talks with a psychiatrist. They helped me to understand the problem and to rationalize it. But while I have
rationalized it thoroughly, I cannot control it. The practice has become continually worse, and now I cannot
even pay proper attention to what goes on in the classroom." We inquired into the boy's home conditions and
found them unfavorable, in that they were conducive to
solitude and idleness. Therefore, instead of discussing
the problem further, we outlined a set of conditions for
dealing with the habit, namely:

A maximum of enforced physical exertion in company
with other men.

A minimum of privacy and a maximum of enforced
social contacts during off hours.

A minimum of free time and a maximum of supervised
time.

These conditions, it will be seen, were calculated to
reduce his opportunities for temptation. But above all,
they were conducive to the constructive use of his energies in developing many new and useful habits, and in
stimulating his interests in more wholesome directions.
A summer camp would meet some of these conditions
but the ordinary camp was not sufficiently strenuous and
allowed too much free time. An intensively conducted
military camp was therefore recommended. The interview had taken about thirty minutes.

When next we saw him, some three months later, he

had just returned from such a camp. Obviously, he had passed the critical point. "I am not yet cured," he said with a smile and a straight look, "but at least I have made a great improvement, and I know now what I must do to improve further." From the point where he was practically without will-power, he had achieved a stage in self-determination, had accepted the responsibility for his own habits, and had some ideas of how to plan his life toward a desired goal.

This was an extreme instance of habit perversion and loss of will-power. Nevertheless in principle it is exactly like innumerable cases of neuroses, both mild and serious, including alcoholism, the innumerable fears, and the sense of inferiority generally. Young people who substitute the reading of fervent love stories for the exertions of dancing and useful forms of social intercourse, who emphasize private and intellectual pursuits at the expense of social disciplines, who resort to artificial stimulants instead of using the constructive stimulants which society supplies, who depend on their families instead of striking out for themselves, are bound to develop bad habits. Moreover, they do so by conscious, often deliberate, choice. They may not appreciate the final consequences of their acts. They may have been improperly trained in childhood. But they know what they are doing at the time. If, years later, they developed a serious complex, it must be dealt with as a conscious problem, not through the hocus-pocus of the subconscious mind and the theory of repressed morbid complexes.

There is a class of disorders of conduct, say many psychiatrists, such as alcoholism, irritability, bad temper, cynicism, despondency, and certain sexual perversions, which are beyond the control of the will and for which, therefore, the individual cannot be held morally responsible. They are derived from repressed complexes and should therefore be treated as sicknesses. "We must distinguish," one says, "between moral disease and sin. The man who deliberately embezzles, gets drunk, gratifies his passions, is in a different category from the alcoholic, the kleptomaniac, the sexual pervert. The former may be drunk because of a depraved and brutish nature, whereas the latter is drunk because of a nature so sensitive that it cannot bear the assaults of life. The drunkard is deliberately sinning, the alcoholic is suffering from a moral disease," which should be treated by psychotherapy.

This is a nice distinction for those who can afford it. In effect, it means that those who can afford psychotherapy or medical treatment may retain the luxury of a super-sensitive nature or an unfortunate moral illness; others are just scoundrels or brutes! It means that those in legal difficulties who can afford alienists or psychiatrists, may be found morally irresponsible and therefore escape the legal consequences of a crime.

The evidences of this trend in our legal procedures are plentiful, and the trend here grows directly out of the broad concept of moral irresponsibility as against moral responsibility. No doubt many individuals reach a stage at which they can no longer control themselves, as in the case of the boy just described; but to attribute these states to morbid complexes, repressions, moral illness, or the subconscious mind, only postpones the program of action by which the individual can acquire the habits of self-control. Human nature is only too ready to find excuses for its mistakes and weakness. Now we furnish a ready-made, pseudo-scientific set of excuses to help people abandon the last vestige of their moral responsibility.

"Everything possible must be done," says a prominent American psychiatrist, "to assist the public to deliver itself from that hangover of the medieval ages that stamped mental troubles as being the result of demoniacal possession or some other nefarious and disgraceful causation." But, although the author of this statement holds a chair and teaches psychiatry in one of the great theological schools, he has nothing to say about the sins of omission or commission which so often result in mental disorder. There are still quite a few people, we find, who do not attribute their problems to the complexities of modern life, but to their own mistakes and selfishness. Such persons are usually easier to help, that is to help themselves, than those who come with the sophisticated naïveté of a helpless victim expecting a painless and even pleasant operation.

As for medieval demons, they are, if anything, preferable to the modern demons—the libido, the censor, dream symbols, the subconscious, an Oedipus complex, inferiority complex, sadism, super-ego, and innumerable others. Here is a passage the like of which may be found in any psychoanalytic journal: "In such persons id impulses, to be expressed toward others, must undergo extensive modification in the super-ego, a process intimately connected with the problem of sadism. Introjection-projection mechanisms play an important role. Moral substitution is most pronounced when original oral-sadistic impulses are displaced upon anal-sadism." From the standpoint of psychology, this is sheer nonsense, compared with which medieval demonology is wholesome.

No doubt there are many cases in which the individual has almost completely lost control of himself. His bad habits so outnumber or overshadow his good habits that he seems to be wholly possessed by evil forces. No amount of analysis or advice can help some of these individuals to regain control of themselves. Only a drastic reconstruction of their habits offers any hope, but they themselves lack the power to undertake such a program. Their situation requires camps or institutions unlike any we now have, and something far removed from the hospitals in which a bed is the principal therapeutic agent.

The institutions I have in mind would combine the complete control of a prison with the disciplines of a military camp and the manual program of a trade or agricultural school. Under such complete measures the individual could be kept so busy and so usefully occupied that he would, in a short time, develop a great collection of new useful habits and skills. As in the case of the young man who went to a military camp, such an organization of the energies is likely to raise individuals to the level where they have regained, or possibly achieved for the first time, the power to determine themselves. The process is the same as that which takes place in developing self-determination in children, and such adults must be treated almost as children until they have acquired enough good habits.

Much harm has been done by the theory that a person's fears are due to some emotional experience in his youth which now acts as an unconscious complex. One of the examples given by Karl Menninger is typical. A young woman was subject to fits of crying whenever she heard running water while in the presence of a particular aunt. It was found that in youth, while walking in the woods, she had fallen and wedged her foot between the rocks in a running brook. She lay half-submerged for hours before her aunt found and rescued her. This terrible experience, apparently forgotten, in later years produced these crying spells. When this experience was discovered and related to her present crying spells, this affliction disappeared.

Instances of this kind have undoubtedly occurred. However, the sensational misuse of these rare cases has led many people to believe that their fears, which take hundreds of forms, could be removed by discovering some ancient but now subconscious experience. They are encouraged, therefore, to blame their difficulties on accident, on the past, on their subconscious mind, in short, on anything but themselves. When we go into the lives of such people we often find, in the course of the first few minutes of conversation, that their present fear or fears had a perfectly normal beginning. They have always acted like the would-be diver who got poised but seldom or never made the plunge. Failing to overcome the many little fears early in life they have now developed one big fear or a collection of big fears.

The problem here is not one of probing the unconscious. This is a waste of time and often injurious. The problem is one of motivating the person to undertake a new program of action. We may have to go back to childhood, but in the sense that the person must now acquire, by practice, certain habits which he failed to practice in his youth.

What is this unconscious mind? As popularly thought of under the influence of psychoanalytic theories, it is a deep, mysterious force which takes unfair advantage of the individual. It is an enemy who creeps up on a person in the dark and lays him low. It is a repository for all those evil forces and impulses of human nature which society is trying to repress.

The psychological definition of the unconscious is much less fantastic. The subconscious is a combination of unexpressed energies and past experiences. It is, above all, the repository of all the habits which the individual has developed. The habits of spelling, writing, arithmetic, talking, working, are filed in the subconscious mind ready to be used at the proper moment. All the habits of an effective personality reside there. If a person has developed an adequate range of skills and habits, in accordance with the psycho-dynamics of personality, then his subconscious energies will express themselves freely through these habits. If not, then these energies are blocked, they exert internal pressure, and may finally emerge in some distorted and abnormal fashion. *If a person consciously takes care of his habits, his subconscious mind will take care of itself.*

At least one school of psychiatry has concentrated its studies on the problems of habit formation, and that is the school under Dr. Adolf Meyer at Johns Hopkins Medical School. Speaking of this school, Dr. L. B. Hohman, associate in psychiatry, says:* "That human reactions are built out of habit integration is really not accepted except in a few quarters. Most of the psychologic world (Dr. Hohman here must mean *psychiatric* or *psychoanalytic* world, since the study of habits has been the very core of psychology for well over fifty years and William James on *Habit* is a classic) still prefer to search for mysterious complexities—calling them the unconscious, the id, the super-ego, etc., or on the other hand looking for inborn, or hereditary, or constitutional obscurities about which we actually have little, and that not definite, knowledge. This search for the mysterious has hindered the treatment and understanding of human problems tremendously. In my experience, even a clear demonstration of the simplicity of correcting behavior problems in children leaves most parents and nearly all doctors and educators unconvinced that a simple mechanism is involved. . . . Children have sets of problem habits rather than problem personalities. . . . Habit sets which can be integrated and disintegrated explain much more than we formerly thought. . . . Emotion patterns can be handled like any other habit patterns." Parents and educators will find Dr. Hohman's complete paper, with its many examples of training children, extremely worth while.

This point of view, which has long been the basis of scientific psychology, will undoubtedly make headway in the psychiatric field as well. In the meanwhile, there remains a wide gap between the psychological concept

* Child Research Clinic of the Woods Schools, Langhorne, Pennsylvania; *Proceedings*, October 1936.

of personality and the dominant medical concept represented by psychiatry, endocrinology, neurology, and psychoanalysis. The latter emphasize the external causes of personality, the glands, intercranial pressure, heredity, medication, psychic surgery, etc. In its concepts of mental causes the emphasis is too often on the subconscious, on prolonged analysis, on sex and other compulsions presumably beyond the individual's control. The tendency is to permit adults to regard themselves as victims of circumstances rather than as responsible agents.

The psychological concept of personality, on the other hand, more often insists on the responsibility of the individual for his habits and resulting difficulties. True, the parents are responsible for the child's early habits. His problems may, therefore, be due to his parents or his early environment, but their solution must come mainly through his own efforts. A minimum of analysis is approved and a maximum of action is urged. Psychological tests are extensively used to measure habits, and programs of action based on the results are suggested; but, while this may seem mechanical, the essential fact is that the individual himself adopts the program and practices the new habits involved. The psychologist insists that, in the final analysis, there can be no machinists of the soul, but that each person must remain the captain of his own soul.

The term *soul*, which I have been using without definition, has no scientific standing. Indeed, no scientific definition of the soul is possible. In my use of the term it refers to something synonymous with the highest value in the individual. I see the soul as a unique power which enables the individual to say: "I do not have to remain as I am, I can be something better. Hereditary influences may not have endowed me richly, but I can make much of what I have. Circumstances may be difficult, but instead of becoming their victim I shall rise above them. My reason may be inadequate but my faith can be strong. I have faith in my powers as a free will agent, able to choose between right and wrong. I have faith in a moral and spiritual order higher than any comprehended by science or reason. By faith I can accept a super-human concept of personality which gives me confidence in my own potentialities. I will not accept defeat, I will struggle to achieve. I may fall but I will rise again. I may not win wealth, but I will win mastery over myself."

VII

PERSONAL SECURITY OR
SOCIAL SECURITY?

VII

PERSONAL SECURITY OR
SOCIAL SECURITY?

"WHAT can I do for a bad case of the jitters?"
The young man who asked this question had begun to worry about himself and his future. His education was finished, college and then a business school. His family had paid all his expenses. They had also set up a trust fund giving him a minimum income of thirty dollars a week for life. This meant social security. He had nothing to fear. He could live indefinitely without working. And yet, he had the jitters. He had tried several jobs and disliked them. He finally concluded, as many never do, that something was wrong with him. He was right.

He had lived in social security at the expense of developing personal security. There had never been any fear of the future in his life, so he had never acquired the courage to face fear and the power to overcome it. In the absence of real fears, he had developed *the fear of fear itself!*

Social security represents something that society or

the family does for the individual. Personal security is something the individual does for himself. The former comes from outside the individual, the latter comes from within. Social security consists largely of things and money given to the individual. Personal security consists of habits and skills which the individual develops for himself and which enable him to be self-sufficient and independent under almost any conditions.

A father became deeply worried about his son. "I have given him every advantage," he grieved, "and now he can't hold a job. He spends his time damning the system and arguing for social justice.

"I myself started life as a day laborer, finally established my own business, and from the profits I was able to give him a good education and a generous allowance. This means nothing to him. In his eyes I am only another capitalist and exploiter of labor. The fact that my enterprise provides a fair living for two hundred families means little to him. I have invited him to learn my business but he will have nothing to do with it. Instead, he has tried to become a writer, but he can't stay in any one place long. Either he becomes fed up with the job or his employer becomes fed up with him. I don't know what to do with him."

"You have already done too much," was our conclusion. "How can you expect your boy to acquire straight habits of thinking when your generosity has always made it unnecessary for him to do anything but theorize? You yourself have discouraged him from thinking about the fundamentals of work and how to earn a living. Reduce his allowance to five dollars a week and tell him that in six months you will stop it entirely. Tell him that if he wants to reform the world instead of himself, he will have to do it with his own earnings, not with your 'ill-gotten' gains."

The personality traits, *self-determination* and *economic self-determination* included in the P.Q. test have already been mentioned. Our nation-wide studies with this test show that children who receive an allowance from their parents as a matter of course tend to have weaker personalities than do children who receive an allowance only for polishing shoes, tending the furnace, making beds, and other family chores. Young people who sell magazines or who obtain jobs from the neighbors, or who work to earn money during summer vacations, we find, tend to have stronger personalities than those who do not. The importance of such activities lies not in the rewards or money received but in the habits and attitudes which they develop. These habits are such as to transform the character of an individual from that of a sponge to that of a giver, from being only a consumer to being also a producer. Hundreds of desirable habits and attitudes may be acquired in the process, such as:

The skills of talking and dealing with people for whom work is being done.

Habits of social initiative, in looking for work, in asking questions or suggesting possibilities.

Powers of concentration in completing a task within the time assigned.

Habits of undertaking tasks which are unpleasant

and uninteresting, through which many new interests and pleasures are developed.

Habits of paying attention to the desires and interests of other people.

Skills in making agreements, and habits of carrying out contracts faithfully.

Habits of self-control and tact in dealing with equals and superiors.

Habits of evaluating money and personal pleasures in terms of the time and energy required to obtain them.

Habits of getting up in the morning and going to bed at night; better habits of sleep and relaxation.

Better sex habits and control of sex energies through the elimination of idle time, and through the devotion of the energies to creative enterprise.

Habits of planning or creating new jobs and services, of finding work instead of waiting for a job to come along.

Straighter habits of thinking about oneself, one's family, and about society at large. For example, instead of acquiring the attitude that the family or society owes the individual a living or an opportunity to make a living, the attitude becomes one of personal responsibility including the obligation to create one's own opportunities.

All of these habits and attitudes are essential to a well-balanced and effective personality.

"My sixteen-year-old boy," a proud father told us, "works in a restaurant near the high school for his luncheon. Saturdays he helps a groceryman make deliveries. His mother scolds me for letting the boy work so hard and causing him to miss what she calls the *higher things of life*. I have a hard time explaining to her that when he works an hour to earn one meal, he is learning one of the greatest of all lessons, the lesson of giving before receiving."

Parents in modest circumstances, and especially parents whose struggles have lifted them a notch higher in the economic scale, so often reason: "I do not want my children to suffer the hardships and privations which I had to suffer. Thank goodness I can give them an education and many advantages which I never had." Little do we realize, in our selfish pride and affection, that we are depriving our children of a priceless birthright, the right to struggle, to suffer and to achieve thereby emotional maturity and the security of a self-supporting personality.

Again and again we find young people lacking in the habits of self-determination and personal security. The cause so often turns out to be the prolonged *wet-nurse* attitude of the parents.

"But," one father remarked, "I have a larger income than I need. Therefore I gave an allowance to my two sons and even increased it when they were married. Both boys have jobs and are doing well. I cannot see that my generosity has hurt them."

Some children have so strong a fiber that almost nothing can hurt them; or their parents train them so well in fundamentals that money cannot spoil their independence. However, our studies of personality show that subsidies tend to be harmful. We have examined many young people with excellent minds, unusual talents, but so disorganized in their sense of values that we have recommended their immediate withdrawal from college and their going to work. Often this has entirely changed their personality and character. Deprived of their social security they developed personal security.

"There are a hundred thousand young people out of work in my city," argued a certain college man. "How do you expect me to get a job under those circumstances?"

"If they all feel the way you do none of them will," we replied. "Finding a job is more than hunting four-leaf clovers or waiting for something to turn up. There are more jobs waiting to be done today than ever in the world's history. Good jobs are becoming more plentiful but competent workers are becoming more scarce."

"What shall America do for its youth?" was the subject for discussion in one of New York City's famous forums not long ago. After some discussion in which speakers had urged provisions for a free college education, subsidies to make possible earlier marriage, the guarantee of interesting jobs with self-supporting wages, and similar arrangements, one young woman remarked: "It seems to me that our subject 'What shall America do for its youth?' should really be: 'What shall our youth do for America and for themselves?' America is already doing more for its youth than any nation in the world, probably far too much. Isn't it time for the youth of America to rebel against the *gimme* idea and consider instead ways of giving?" The original subject of this forum grows out of the concept of social security. The proposed subject represents the ideals of personal security and personal responsibility.

The decay of personality and character, especially in America, is very largely due to the subsidies which a higher economic standard of living has enabled parents to give their children. What families have done, a civilization of plenty is now attempting to do for its citizens at large.

By substituting social paternalism for personal responsibility, governmental subsidies for private initiative, the principle of redistributing wealth for that of creating wealth, the personalities of multitudes have been undermined. Increasingly this mistaken concept creates individuals who are dependent upon society rather than on themselves. The inevitable result is spineless characters and puny personalities.

No decent society will allow its people to starve, but the belief that society owes every person a job or the opportunity to work will not only ruin the individuals who hold it but the society which acts on it as well. The individual who accepts this belief is like the adult child who continues to live on a benevolent family. His economic security is bought at the price of emotional and intellectual integrity. The longer his family supports him, the longer he waits for a suitable opportunity to arise, the less he is fitted to go out and create one.

A nation which promises to support its citizens automatically and which encourages them to wait for the jobs to which they have a right, will find its population increasingly unfit either to get or to hold jobs.

In the midst of great unemployment, one can find a family of five adults, four of whom are gainfully employed. Near by there will be a similar family of five, all of whom are without work. Is this a matter of economics or of personality? The members of the first family are probably more enterprising and industrious. In a marginal situation they are both willing and able to give some employer a better service for the wages he can afford to pay. Therefore even when jobs are scarce, many have jobs not because they absolutely need them, but because they have better personalities or capacities than those who remain unemployed. Even in this situation the opportunities for jobs or for rendering gainful services are conditioned not by what people *need* but by what they can *give*.

Jobs do not exist by right or by principle, but only as effective personalities create them. They cannot be made artificially by business at large nor guaranteed by labor unions. Not even a government can create jobs for long except under certain conditions. In a dictatorship or under fascism jobs can be given to every worker. But then the workers become the slaves of the state. They must take the jobs assigned them, together with the hours, the conditions, and the wages which go with them.

In a democracy of free individuals, this freedom also involves the responsibility of creating jobs. Every individual must contribute to this process. To me, one of the heroic outcomes of the depression were the many apple stands and flower stands which dotted the city; one of its tragedies the extent to which wholesale and indiscriminate relief discouraged these initial efforts. Far more effective work in creating jobs would have been done if people had not been encouraged to wait for jobs to grow up of their own accord.

One of America's great business men, at the age of twenty-one, found himself in the middle of a depression, without a job, money or prospects. With thousands of others he stood daily in the breadlines common in that day. "I was more worried about the depression in my mind than about the depression in my finances. Associating with the unemployed made me feel still worse. So I tramped out into the country. It was late fall and there was little work. Finally one farmer let me sleep and eat on his place for any odd jobs I could do. He had little money and could pay me nothing. I found so many jobs to do that I stayed for two years. I really helped that farmer to make some money. When I left he gave me one hundred dollars. That was my first capital and it started me in business."

Two years without minimum wages or maximum hours! Two years of learning how to give more than he got! Today he is a millionaire restaurant owner, still giving people what they want. Contrast this experience with the case of a W.P.A. painter who was given a regular job. After five days his employer was forced to let him go. "I have an estimate to meet for this job," the employer explained, "and at the rate you are working it will cost fifty percent more to finish the job than I can collect. You seem to know your trade. What makes you so slow?"

"I was afraid," replied the W.P.A. worker, "that the

quicker I finished the job the sooner I would be out of work again."

It has been repeatedly proclaimed that the fear of social insecurity is creating a nation of neurotics and undermining the personalities of people. Psychologically, there is only a small gap between fear and action. In the face of fear, people can become either paralyzed and lie down, or they can become more active, more determined, more creative than before. A little influence, one way or the other, may tip the scales. Our great leaders chose to tip the scales in favor of permanent fear. Our more able and intellectual population, having cultivated the habits of subsidizing their children, readily rationalized this vice in the idealism of social security for all. The result has been all those sweeping, cash-register methods for taking care of people automatically.

All these devices are attempts to create security from without, that is, in the individual's environment rather than in himself. Therefore all of them are bound to fail. They palliate an outward fear at the expense of the inner experience of conquering that fear. Their effect on personality will be exactly like the effects of a repeated opiate, larger and larger doses will become necessary. To the extent that such measures seem to succeed temporarily, the fears and insecurity they will produce finally will be all the more devastating. Not only the weak but the strong will suffer, because as dependency increases, the productiveness of the able must decrease. Social security can be no more secure than the sum total of the personal security of all its constituents.

The powerful appeal which the ambitious plans for

social security make to the popular imagination is eloquent proof of the extent to which the characters and personalities of a nation have already decayed. Only a population of weaklings, of parents who are bringing up their children as weaklings, of adults too depraved to desire the responsibility of taking care of their old folks, would be willing to sacrifice their independence and moral integrity to such a paternalism. The complete failure of our educational system to educate its pupils in the fundamental truths and practices of an effective personality is nowhere more dramatically revealed than in the headlong scramble for social security.

The belief that people can achieve social security by voting for it has become the foremost superstition in the United States.

Social *in*security stimulates the individual to action, to struggle, and thus to progress. Social security lulls people into a state of stagnation which develops finally into a case of jitters. Social security develops in time the very fears and doubts it was intended to allay.

SUBSIDIZED MARRIAGE

The practice of subsidizing children and giving them an education and many other free privileges is a natural result of growing economic abundance. Parents have come to indulge their children without thinking, and largely because they were able to do so. In recent years, however, this unconscious practice has been converted into a social theory which expresses itself in many forms. One of these is that young people should be encouraged to marry even before they can afford to support themselves. The delays in marriage imposed by our modern civilization or by economic conditions are claimed to be injurious, therefore parents should help their children to set up housekeeping and even the state should come to their aid if they have babies. Many prominent sociologists, psychiatrists, and, I regret to say, even some psychologists, have publicly urged this plan.

In so many cases of unhappy marriage, which have come under our observation, the chief cause has been the fact that the marriage was subsidized by the parents. The effects of subsidized marriage are especially serious in the case of the husband or wage-earner. The most powerful incentive to his achievement of economic competence has been removed. He has, so to speak, been given the prize without having had to run the race. An artificial set of circumstances has been created representing a short-cut to happiness. Even after marriage he does not have to face reality. Instead of relying wholly on himself, and developing the habits of personal competence, he falls back on the financial crutch which has been given him. When, as sometimes happens, this crutch is taken from him, his personality may have disintegrated to the point of almost complete helplessness and insecurity.

Parents who subsidize the marriage of their children, no matter what the justification, assume a terrific responsibility. They virtually place themselves between their children and reality, and deprive them of the joint struggle to create their own economic and emotional security. No large-scale psychological studies have yet been devoted to this specific problem. The indications are that such studies, when made, will show divorce and failure much higher among subsidized marriages than among marriages which were not subsidized.

Early marriage is usually desirable, but only when the couple undertakes also the full financial responsibility even at the sacrifice of an accustomed standard of living.

BATHROOMS AND PERSONALITIES

Jobs in a democracy are created in the last analysis by the ingenuity, the enterprise, and the determination of the entire population, both the employed and the unemployed. This is true whatever the economic fluctuations and mechanics of an industrial people, or the effects of technological advances, or the temporary expedients to alleviate or spread unemployment. The strength of democracy lies in the freedom and determination of its millions of independent personalities, not in the all-wise planning of a few. Our popular leaders, instead of inspiring the millions to use their powers and to rely on themselves, spread intellectual doctrines which encourage them to excuse themselves, to blame such abstractions as business or the economic system, and to wait for the cushions of social security. What parents in an excusable love have too often done for their children, the fathers of a nation, prompted by academic fallacies, are now doing for their countrymen.

The deepest of all fallacies, however, is the assertion that personalities can be improved merely by raising the standard of living. This doctrine has been adopted by many of the new school of sociologists. Their logic is somewhat as follows: The percentage of crimes committed by people living in the slum districts is much higher than that for the people living under better housing conditions. Therefore poor housing conditions are responsible for crime!

The possibility that people continue to live or move into these districts because their ideals, characters, and personalities are weak in the first place does not seem to occur to these sociologists. The frequency of crime today as compared with thirty years ago, when living standards were much lower, receives little or no consideration.

Sex crimes and other crimes costing the government millions of dollars could be drastically reduced, claims a Chicago professor of sociology, through federal aid in a national housing program. Incipient criminals, he claims, are incubated in the squalid housing conditions of our cities. In fifty-eight of our largest cities about one in five homes have no inside toilet facilities; about one in four are without bathrooms; one in three are without running hot water; some fifty percent are heated by stoves in rooms and halls instead of by a central heating plant; one in eight are overcrowded. "Such living conditions," he concludes, "turn men into beasts; make them like their fellow animals of jungle-town—marauding, predatory, rapacious, and lustful."

Speaking as a student who visited several New York tenement districts in 1912 with Professor Bailey, one of the great sociologists of the old school, the tenements described above are palaces in comparison. Moreover, a few who read this, like the writer, were probably brought up with the washtub as a bathtub, without hot running water, without a central heating plant, and without an inside toilet. From the standpoint of the psychology of habit formation, such conditions are less conducive to the formation of bad sex habits than are the more comfortable modern homes.

There are so many things that can be done to help people improve their personalities without subsidizing them directly or just giving them things. Playgrounds for the young have already been emphasized. The C.C.C. camps are another good example. Similarly whole families could be put into model communities for a month or more and taught how to cook, how to keep a house clean, how to eat, how to keep regular hours, and how to discipline children.

One of the greatest bars to the development of personal security is petty gambling in the form of sweepstakes, lotteries, numbers, etc. Gambling represents an attempted short-cut to wealth, an attempt to achieve something without developing the habits of work or rendering a corresponding service. Gambling is bad enough for those who have achieved competence or who can afford speculation. However, it is especially prevalent among the poor and the idle, many of whom chronically devote their occasional earnings to this pursuit. And yet, while we have passed sweeping laws for social security and relief, this vicious enemy of personal security flourishes unchecked and is even fostered in high places.

The improvements in personality and character never

come from *things* as such; in fact quite the contrary, as all history proves. Personality develops by learning how to use things, especially time, energy, and money, how to create things, including the homely services of living and coöperation with others. Every old-fashioned and experienced social worker knows that the most precious ingredient in a family's possession is its independence and self-respect, and that these are to be cherished and developed rather than undermined by well-meant charity. This concept has been systematically and mechanically destroyed in recent years. For the ideal of personal security we have substituted the mirage of social security.

EDUCATED CHILDREN

There was a time when the children of the most privileged classes had to contribute their labors toward the family economy. Today this is not only unnecessary among the rich, who shower their children with luxuries and privileges; it is even made difficult among the comparatively poor. Instead of well-to-do parents, a society rich in taxes thrusts upon children with little regard for their fitness, the luxury of an academic education including a high school and even a college education. Society condemns children, with an increasing lack of discrimination, to spend the critical years of their development in acquiring a free education. The trend of the times is to make this education freer and freer, to subsidize children more and more.

Step by step, especially in the United States, children

are being deprived of the opportunities to develop the habits of economic self-sufficiency. The president of a great eastern college recently condemned the "work your way through college" theory as more destructive than productive. In other institutions and sections of the country similar opinions are being expressed. More scholarships and wider financial assistance for an increasing number of students are being constantly provided. Through high school and the critical years of adolescence, and through college, indulgent parents and a society of indulgent citizens are turning their children into sponges instead of producers. Education has become our biggest luxury, with a $10,000,000,000 plant, a $2,-500,000,000 annual cost, and the end not yet in sight.

And yet, our great educational system, while subject to increasing criticism, is hardly ever condemned for this disastrous weakness, that is, the extent to which it delays the development of habits of economic self-sufficiency. Quite the contrary, it is often condemned for a tendency toward vocational training at the expense of culture. This is the substance of the extensive criticisms by that well-known educator, Robert M. Hutchins. "Our schools and even our colleges," he states, "are concerned less and less with teaching students how to think and more and more with teaching them the tricks of a trade." The primary purpose of education, he believes, is the development of the mind, not merely in relation to a trade but in relation to life generally. He considers this especially important because the rapid changes in our social order make it desirable to prepare students to take care of themselves in any set of circumstances.

This academic concept of education betrays a disregard of the psychology of the mind and personality. A person untrained to take care of himself in one situation is still less prepared to take care of himself in all situations. Moreover, every psychologist working with people knows that a man who has a trade, a job, a wife and family, even though he has only a grade school education, is a straighter and saner thinker than a college graduate or Ph.D. who has no job, who is not prepared for practical life, not able to support a family, and therefore emotionally unbalanced and eager to change the entire economic system. A vocation and economic independence, our studies show, is the core which unifies all the other habits of personality. Without this, the mind and personality are likely to be disorganized.

The difference between childhood and adulthood has been described in many ways. Psychologically I should say that the person becomes an adult at the point when he produces more than he consumes or earns more than he spends. This may be at the age of eighteen, twenty-five or thirty-five. Some people remain unproductive and dependent children forever and therefore intellectually and emotionally immature.

One great foundation decided to invest its funds in the education of mature young people. Generous scholarships are given to young men and women who, after graduating from high school, have been working and supporting themselves for two years. A variation of this principle of education, the principle of *work and learn,* was pioneered and successfully developed by Dean Schneider at the University of Cincinnati. It is embodied in the Antioch College plan, the Hershey Industrial School, all medical education including nursing, and, most promising of all, in the C.C.C. camps. In my opinion, this principle must become a universal one, applied in suitable forms to all education, if education is to become more a preparation for life and less a preparation for vicious leisure and wishful thinking.

VIII

THE PSYCHOLOGY OF SPORTS-
MANSHIP

VIII

THE PSYCHOLOGY OF SPORTS-
MANSHIP

THE class of 1912 of Vassar College recently published certain facts about its members. After twenty-five years 65 percent of the 229 graduates had been married. Among the Phi Beta Kappa or high scholarship group only 61 percent had married. "But if she was one of our beauties," the report states, "one of our daisy chain or a class marshal, her chances would shoot up to 80 percent. Still you must not think that beauty leads the race, for the athletes are really at the top. If she were a member of one of our teams or even a sub, her chances of marriage would be 83 percent. And if she happened to be on the hockey team, her chances would be 90 percent."

Our studies of personality have shown that competitive athletic sports make a major contribution toward the development of an effective personality. The facts just given represent one more bit of evidence in the growing list of evidences confirming this discovery. These girl athletes may not have been brilliant conversationalists, but they had learned some of the lessons of teamwork and good sportsmanship. So many people today think of personality in terms of the ability to talk well. The popular literature on developing personality usually concerns itself chiefly with teaching people how to talk. From a psychologist's point of view, this emphasis on speech is often more harmful than helpful. It tends to make people self-conscious, more hesitant and analytical. Are they saying the right thing at the right time, according to the proper rule, and is the other person aware of the mechanism?

EFFECTS ON PERSONALITY

In advising people about personality problems we never dwell on the mechanics of conversation supposed to make them popular. Instead, we often suggest that they join certain group activities, especially competitive games. In the excitement of the game, in concentrating on the play and the rules, they will forget themselves. And when the individual forgets himself, then he is likely to talk naturally and to the point. If he forgets himself too far, his fellow players may correct him much more directly and naturally than they would in less exciting situations. In this rapid-fire, give-and-take process many social skills are acquired in a natural fashion. The intervals of relaxation and the after-glow of the game are notably conducive to easy conversation.

All kinds of group activities in which people work or play together are conducive to the development of personality. The conversation which grows naturally out of such activities is far more effective than is the power of speaking developed for its own sake. There may not be so much of it, but what there is will be more closely related to action, to worthwhile achievement.

Why should competitive athletic games contribute so much to personality? In the first place because a person expends usually two or three times the energy used in solitary pursuits. The stimulus of competition urges players to their utmost exertion. This lavish use of the energies tends to reduce, immediately, one of the chief causes of emotional and mental tension, of fears and worries. We have urged thousands of neurotic men and women and children to undertake the practice of tennis, badminton, basketball, hockey, and other appropriate games, with excellent results.

In these days of easy living, of pills and soporifics, of psychiatric patter about neurotic ailments and their obscure causes, the good old-fashioned catharsis of strenuous physical exertion is not only forgotten but looked on with contempt. Our mechanized civilization has increasingly done away with hard work, especially for children, and among the poor almost as much as among the rich. Competitive sports may almost be regarded as the modern substitute for physical labor. However, the statistics of athletic sports throughout America indicate that we are becoming increasingly a nation of spectators or sitters. The spectacle of America crowding the stadiums, or listening to the reports of games over the radio, has been likened to the decadent days of Rome. The facts are infinitely more ominous. The populace of Rome at least had to walk to the games.

The measure of a college or university today is too

often its stadium and its football team. Athletics in the colleges have been prostituted to the demands of Roman holidays. The majority of students participate only casually or in their spare time, while a chosen few participate in a manner which often does them more harm than good. Commercial competitive athletics tend to develop in players an exaggerated and one-sided sense of superiority, and among spectators a vicarious and anæsthetic feeling of satisfaction.

When I was in college, we used to feel sorry for the minor teams which had to play their own matches on the day of an important football game. Now I realize that we should have pitied ourselves, who were able to be spectators. The extremes of competitive sports for the few should not be allowed to obscure their value for the many. If participated in by all rather than by a few, games would be played more for the good of the players and less for the sake of an audience.

Within a block of my birthplace, on the site of a useful reservoir, a great public stadium has been built as a W.P.A. project. It provides seats for 50,000 spectators. The funds required to build it would have made possible probably ten well equipped playgrounds for the city's youth. One of the major sociological discoveries in recent years is that city areas well equipped with playgrounds have definitely fewer delinquent children than are found in areas without playgrounds. Delinquency and juvenile crime have become a great national problem. "Of our fourteen million petty crimes each year," says J. Edgar Hoover, "a majority is committed by persons of less than voting age. Over twenty-four percent of our murderers, our rapists, our arsonists, burglars, extortionists, bank-robbers and kidnapers are so young that they may still be technically called children."

On all sides we hear proposals for educating the youth against crime. One proposal made in respect to a boy of twelve who had been in several difficulties with the police was to send him to the museums to keep him off the streets and get him interested in things cultural. The parents tried this suggestion and the boy made daily trips to an art museum with evident enjoyment. Before long a Buddhist household shrine valued at several thousand dollars was found missing and its theft traced to this boy. His appreciation of art had turned into an impulse for possession.

This incident is unusual but the theory of education it represents is quite common. This theory is that character and personality can be developed and crime prevented through books, talks, classroom studies, in short through academic procedures. Dozens of psychological studies have already shown that there is little or no relationship between personality and years of education. The well educated are as likely to be socially maladjusted as are the less educated.

The term *crime* suggests the term *character* because character usually means freedom from crime. The strong character can resist the temptation to do wrong, even though he is not well adjusted or successful. The strong personality finds crime unnecessary because he has learned to live and work within the social order. The term *personality*, as I use it, does not exclude character but does include more positive and energetic qualities.

Athletic sports have a positive character-building value. The energies of youth must have outlets, and sports provide such outlets not only in a wholesome but in a socialized fashion. Here the concepts of self-control, of obeying the rules, of sportsmanship and consideration for others, are taught in actual practice. Here the pressures of a group on the individual represent twenty teachers in action as compared to one discussing lawful behavior in the abstract.

PRACTICAL SEX EDUCATION

The academic approach to behavior problems has become notorious in the field of sex education. Both in respect to children and adults our civilization has come to treat sex as an intellectual problem. In my work with adults I have come to the conclusion that those who appreciate sex normally do not talk much about it, whereas those who talk about it most, usually understand it least. Psychoanalysts and many psychiatrists are professionally preoccupied with sex. If our civilization had less time to talk about sex problems, there would be fewer sex problems to talk about.

A mother called us on the telephone one day and in great anxiety told about discovering some salacious stories and pictures hidden away in the room of her sixteen-year-old boy. Would we talk to her boy about this dangerous practice? We said, Certainly not. What could we advise? We suggested a comprehensive examination of his habits and activities, his aptitudes and interests. Such an examination, requiring about ten hours, was made. The boy was found to be under-developed in his social interests and activities. However, he had during the past year shown a decided interest in his physical development, and through gymnastic exercises had considerably improved a rather weak physique. With this as a starting point, we mapped out with him a program including competitive sports in the execution of which the school was asked to coöperate.

To motivate the boy further, we discussed the psychodynamics of energy and its conversion into the skills of personality. Incidentally, we pointed out that the idle discussion of sex matters and the attention to certain kinds of literature and pictures tended to stimulate the energies in wasteful directions, and hindered their translation into socially useful habits. Some interest in such objects, we explained, could be taken for granted and was quite normal. The important question was a program of action for the constructive use of the energies. Such a program, if followed, would help to put problems of sex as well as other problems in their proper place. This approach, in the main, applies also to young people and unmarried adults preoccupied with questions of sex.

Children should be given quite definite information about the mechanics of sex before the age of eight. This is a task of fifteen minutes or so. The major problem in sex education is one of developing the energies into a sufficient variety of social habits and skills of a kind involving both sexes. In this process, competitive athletic sports and social dancing are of major importance.

Aside from this, the emphasis in sex education should be on the parents, that is on the disciplines they should enforce regarding the movies, reading matter, allowances, late hours, the use of automobiles, etc. The age of puberty necessitates some further discussion, but a minimum amount if proper basic habits have been formed.

SPEEDY LEARNING

The value of competitive sports goes far beyond the physical exertion involved. In such pursuits the individual acquires new habits and skills much more quickly than in many other situations. The stimulus of competition, the constant example of others, the unusual energy exerted, greatly speed up the process of learning. Dr. L. J. O'Rourke, one of the country's foremost psychologists, has demonstrated that this applies even to the mastery of English usage. He has found that English grammar, when taught in the form of a playground sport, with the children divided into two competing teams, is learned at least five times more quickly than by the individualistic method of the traditional classroom. In fact, children who seem slow or stupid in class often learn the same subject with remarkable speed on the playfield.

For this reason we so often advise people in need of better social habits to participate in group activities. We know that such activities will develop the desired habits quickly and naturally. A person may get hints about playing tennis or golf from a book, but he learns best by actually playing. Just so, a person may learn the theories of dealing with people by reading, but he acquires the skills most quickly in situations where people deal with him both roughly and sympathetically.

COÖPERATION VS. COMPETITION

The greatest value of competitive sports, however, lies in its lessons of coöperation and teamwork. There cannot even be competition except through perfect coöperation. In every possible way imaginable, coöperation comes first, competition can only follow. The youth, participating in a competitive sport, must say to himself in effect: "Now I am going to practice and play this game, not according to my ideas but according to the rules and customs of the game. I will do not as I please but as the coach and the team please. When they say 'Practice' I will practice whether I feel like it or not. When they say 'Do it this way and not that way,' I will try whether I agree or not. If I get bumped or am scolded unjustly, I will not cry or quarrel but keep on trying. If I get into a match game and the umpire gives me what I am sure is a raw decision, I will not stage a sit-down strike but be a good sport. In short, I am going to learn this game so that I can serve and help my teammates. In time they may want me to play with them regularly and I shall enjoy playing."

One of the prevailing academic fads among drawing-room sociologists is to urge coöperation in place of competition, and to condemn our competitive democracy as conducive to selfishness and moral depravity. It takes highly educated people to reverse the *a b c*'s of history and human nature to this extent. Competition is the very fuel and power of coöperation. Competition represents the force in every individual which makes coöperation necessary. The coöperation between the members of a team or of a business is raised to its nth powers, as is also the coöperation between members of other teams or companies, because of the competition which motivates them all.

Competition and consequent coöperation are inevitable in the nature of man, even in the religious concept of the striving soul. The practical question is: What forms of competition and coöperation are conducive to personality and social harmony?

The most extensive and complete types of coöperation, historically, have been shown by nations at war. Patriotism is the slogan for the sacrifice of all lesser competitions and personal interests. In war, regimentation and collectivism, both voluntary and enforced, reach their highest point. The rules and laws of all ordinary living are suspended to make possible the supreme coöperative effort.

Thus we have the tragic paradox that coöperation at its peak, namely in war, represents destruction at its worst. Here we have competition not under a set of rules but without any rules, not for the sake of the game but to win the game at any cost. The methods of warfare have become fouler and fouler and the rules in regard to non-combatants and combatants as well have been progressively abandoned.

What a contrast between this type of coöperation and

that represented by the teams of nations in the Olympic Games!

Even when teams are competing for victory, the rules of coöperation are more important than winning the game. In a football game between Dartmouth and Yale recently, Dartmouth made what seemed like the winning touchdown of a close game. While the Dartmouth stands were still in a frenzy of joy, the ball was brought back by the referee and the Dartmouth team penalized five yards for off-side play. On the next play Dartmouth was again penalized five yards. Then, immediately, another penalty of five yards was measured off for some infringement of the rules. Beginning with a touchdown from the four-yard line, Dartmouth found itself without a touchdown on the nineteen-yard line, entirely through penalties, and still the game went on!

This is coöperation of the highest order, seldom seen in any field of life except competitive sports. Even individual players, in tennis, in track, in golf, submit themselves to the rigors and rules of the game which are more important than their competitive efforts. Competition is always subordinate to coöperation. Winning the game is always secondary to observing the rules of the game and the traditions of sportsmanship.

This voluntary subordination of himself by the individual to the rules and disciplines of the game constitutes the great virtue of competitive sports. He accepts these rules and traditions as they are, not as he thinks they should be. Having accepted them, he confines his energies and thinking to acquiring skills within these limits for coöperation. Instead of spending his time in talk and argument he spends it in action. It is as though, for the time being, *large sections of his frontal lobes or higher brain centers had been removed, but in a wholesome and voluntary manner.* With tremendous concentration and energy he can now strive to acquire mastery of himself and the skills of the sport, the skills of smooth team-play and of sportsmanlike competition. Nowhere does coöperation reach a higher point of effectiveness than here, where all the players voluntarily accept the same rules.

Above all, through submitting himself to this form of regimentation, that is the traditions and rules of the game, the player emerges as a more competent and independent individual. He has won the confidence of his team-mates or the respect of his competitors, and therefore won confidence in himself. By subordinating himself, he has achieved personal superiority. He may, as a winner or a star, achieve individuality in its highest form, the individuality which rests on the willing coöperation of his competitors and team-mates. He has learned the greatest of all principles of personality, that the individual in order to find himself must first lose himself; he must lose himself in the codes of the game and the interests of the larger group. He must put sportsmanship above personal triumph.

And yet, in spite of the fact that competitive athletics exemplify the principles of personality in their highest form, many people regard such activities as an incidental, a secondary, a wholly unnecessary part of life and education. Indeed, our entire educational system implies that competitive games are a lower form of life as compared with the higher intellectual pursuits. Parents and educators deplore the dangers of over-stimulation, of physical and nervous exhaustion. Many children are considered too high-strung and nervous for physical games. Parents pride themselves on their scholastically brilliant children who have no use for athletics. If they believe in competitive sports themselves, they may regret the lack of this interest in their children, but do nothing to overcome it. The nervous, the high-strung, the studious, the indifferent children are just the children who usually need these disciplines most.

HOW FOLLOWERS BECOME LEADERS

Two scientists recently completed a fascinating and revealing study of high school children and their activities.* In three high schools forty outstanding leaders and forty non-leaders were selected. A study of the extra-curricular activities of these two groups revealed that each leader averaged participation in 6.8 activities compared with 1.7 activities for non-leaders. The most frequent extra-curricular activities among leaders were competitive athletics. An analysis of the leisure time of these two groups showed that the leaders found twice as much spare time as did the non-leaders, in spite of the fact that they engaged in four times as many extra-curricular activities. The authors attributed this to the likelihood that leadership rests on planning, foresight, a

* Morpheus Smith and W. C. Nystrom, "A Study of Social Participation and of Leisure Time of Leaders and Non-Leaders," *Journal of Applied Psychology*, June, 1937.

more orderly arrangement of ideas, and a more integrated and efficient life organization generally. Conversely, the non-leaders frittered their time away, although they reported more time spent in reading and solitary activities than did the leaders.

"The fact that leaders participate in games and in attending parties is highly significant," state the authors. "In games the leader gains more experience with people, and this experience is useful to him in leadership. His present leadership may be the outgrowth of such activities in the past."

Most dramatic is the light cast by this study on the oft-made remark: "We cannot all be leaders. Some of us must be followers." This study showed that the leaders were also the good followers, whereas the non-leaders were the poor followers. That is, most of the leaders were not captains or managers, but just members of a team or squad or cast. A leader might be a captain or top-leader in one activity, but was merely a follower in five or six other activities. The members of the non-leader group were followers in only one or two activities or none.

In short, conspicuous leadership in one activity was based on having become a well-disciplined follower in several activities. In the main, the group chosen as the leaders were mostly good followers, and were tolerated as leaders *because they were good followers*. Whereas the non-leader group were not even good followers. All these findings confirm the results of our P.Q. study and the analysis of the psychology of sports given above.

The principles exemplified by competitive sports are

the principles that apply to the development of personality and leadership in any field whatsoever. The musician must subordinate his energies to the practice of scales and exercises, which are the techniques of the game developed by the great masters. In playing either as an individual or in an orchestra, the score represents the rules of the game and the conductor is the captain. Even the artist, regarded as the exponent of originality and individuality, must acquire a mastery of form and accepted techniques before he can be more than a freak. Every science has its laws which all scientists must accept and master in order to achieve competence and the respect of their colleagues. Business has its codes and disciplines, under which the individual must learn to be a good team-mate, a good employee, before he can be a boss or an employer. New labor unions are discovering that they cannot succeed except by subordinating their immediate desires to codes and contracts.

MARRIAGE AND DIVORCE

However, while the rules and disciplines of competitive games have been developed to higher and higher levels, the codes and morals in nearly every other phase of life have been increasingly lowered or discarded. Whereas coöperation in competitive sports has been codified to the point which makes international Olympic Games successful, the codes of sportsmanship in the commonest relationships of life have been degraded.

The morals and laws of marriage are an example. Marriage and the family represent a coöperative-competitive game in life far more important than the games of sport. However, the partner contracting marriage often enters to win only according to his own rules. If, by his purely personal ideas of happiness, he considers himself the loser, he can withdraw from the game. Moreover, the legal rules of marriage have degenerated into laws for divorce. These laws say in effect: "You enter this game to play only so long as you win, or think you are winning; as soon as you begin to lose you may quit, no matter how long you have been married, no matter how many children there are, how much damage may be done to one of the partners, or to the children, or to society."

When the two mothers disputing the possession of a child were brought before Solomon, he ordered the child to be cut in two and one half given to each mother. This threat saved the child and gave him to his true mother. Our divorce proceedings literally cut the children in half, emotionally, mentally, morally, and economically. It is bad enough for children to lose one parent, but our courts often doom them to live a divided life, divided between parents whose affections represent one of the cruellest forms of selfishness. This is not sportsmanship but its very opposite. This is the principle of winning a game at any cost, the principle that one's personal happiness or goal justifies the means. This is the principle of living one's own life regardless of the rest of the team. Instead of codes which put teamwork above personal gratification, as in the competitive sports, our laws do exactly the opposite.

The poor sportsmanship so prevalent in respect to

marriage and the family is one of the basic causes undermining our civilization. It not only affects the personalities of those divorced, but does infinite and often
irreparable damage to the personalities of children. We
have seen it again and again in children whom we have
examined. A recent survey in New York City showed
that more than seventeen percent of the school population of almost 150,000 children, come from *broken
homes*. It was reported that this condition, whether
caused by natural or artificial factors, by death or divorce, took a devastating toll in thwarted personalities
and youthful failures. In comparison with children from
normal homes, these children revealed strong feelings of
insecurity and inferiority. They also possessed an inferior code of ethics and manifested feelings of despondency, extreme cynicism, and a general inability to cope
with normal problems. Obviously, just as the disciplines
of teamwork create personality, so the absence of these
disciplines injures personality.

We are not concerned here with making a case against
divorce but rather with making a case for personality.
Divorce may be justified in certain circumstances. The
significant fact is that our civilization has been more
concerned with justifying divorce than it has been with
codifying the morals and rules for a successful marriage.
We have given our attention to the so-called liberalizing
of the divorce laws, that is, the techniques for breaking
up the game, and failed to develop the rules for better
coöperation or for keeping the game going.

The underlying cause of this trend lies in the popular
philosophy of self-expression, the doctrine that the indi-

vidual must live his own life, that inhibitions and suppressions are harmful, that he must interpret the rules of life according to his own understanding or conscience, that is to say, not literally as in sports, but liberally in accord with his own experience and modern trends. This is the philosophy of poor sportsmanship. This is the philosophy which permits one member of a family to break up the team and to do irreparable damage to its members in order that he may achieve his selfish desires.

A better civilization will codify the disciplines of sportsmanship in marriage, and one of its basic principles will be that the welfare of immature children is, if anything, more important than the imaginary happiness of a parent.

PROGRESSIVE EDUCATION

Not only has our civilization failed in perfecting the morals and codes for the games of life, it has devoted its great intellectual powers to tearing them down. The central trend of liberal education has been to encourage every student to develop his own code in respect to marriage, government, business, labor, international relationships, religion, etc. Therefore, instead of an increasing agreement at least in respect to fundamental rules, we have educated people to greater and greater disagreement in respect to both fundamentals and details. This trend spells the death of coöperation, of competition, of sportsmanship, of personality.

This educational trend has now been given formal expression in the theories and practices of progressive education. Undoubtedly progressive education will make some valuable contributions to methods of teaching, but its central emphasis today is on self-expression at the expense of social disciplines. Self-expression represents the process of learning by experience and through voluntary interests. Social disciplines represent the accumulated experience of the race. Social disciplines are like the rules of a game which children must accept in order that their self-expression may not become disorder. To be sure, the prevalent uncertainty in respect to the proper social disciplines is conducive to a theory of education which tends to break down those we still have.

The conflict between the concepts of self-expression and social disciplines was well stated by the superintendent of schools in a community noted for its fine progressive schools. At a recent meeting of parents this educator spoke somewhat as follows: "Both as a result of the complaints of many parents and as a result of our own experience as educators, we have come to the conclusion that certain phases of progressive education are unsound. As you know, our schools have been operating on the principle that children develop best when their natural and voluntary interests are engaged, and when they are given a considerable range of freedom in expressing these interests. We have assumed that the classroom disciplines generated by these activities would be more effective than the old-fashioned disciplines imposed by teachers from without. Moreover, we have entrusted the children with a large measure of self-government, in the study halls, the cafeteria, and school affairs generally. The results have been, as we all know, a failure among many children to master the routine subjects and to develop the habits of close application to unpleasant but necessary assignments. Noisy and disorderly classrooms have become common, and even the orderly child has been hampered by less orderly classmates.

"We have come to the conclusion that we, as educators, have no reason for existence unless we know more about what is good for children than they know themselves. We have no right to expect them to develop their own disciplines, except under the disciplines which we already know are good and which we must impose as our responsibility. Our program henceforth will be to teach them what is necessary and good for them, in the manner good for them, whether they like it or not. We are not going back to the opposite extreme of harsh dictation, but we are going to subordinate the techniques of self-expression to certain disciplines in the classroom and to the disciplines of the basic subjects."

The theory of self-expression reaches a high point in a set of experimental textbooks recently issued by a commission of the Progressive Education Association. These books, dealing with the "higher morality" are intended for use in high schools. They were prompted by the understandable belief that "some vital spark has been missing in our great educational machine," as evidenced by a "restless and turbulent younger generation mostly surprisingly ignorant or surprisingly well versed in things that aren't so. The ugly proof of this ignorance is sprawled boldly across the records of our courts, our social welfare agencies, and our schools. It is not by chance that crime is most prevalent in the age group just above that of high school. That is the age when most youngsters first meet life and the shock is too much for them." With this thought in mind, these books divest the higher morality of "superstitions, habits and customs, racial superstitions and economic frustrations." Children are told to reason out and decide for themselves certain moral questions, such as pre-marital chastity, which should be the property of the race and not original problems in human geometry.

The text on "Society and Family Life" states that the majority of beliefs which prevail today are traditional and no longer fit the present situation. "We live in an airplane age and retain our ox-cart images. We have a cultural hangover which is giving our society a terrible headache. . . . Such conflicts will continue to arise until we have learned to dump overboard those traditional notions which are out of joint with our own times." Aside from the fact that psychologists are finding so many of our modern beliefs not only untrue but ruinous to personality, and many of the ancient traditions fundamentally sound, such generalizations are quite in keeping with the trends of progressive education. No wonder that the vital spark is missing, or that our younger generation is restless, turbulent, and given to crime!

In wholesome contrast with the egocentric tendencies of progressive education is the contemporary announcement of the New York State Department of Education which makes competitive athletics a regular part of the school curriculum. "For the first time athletic sports are placed on the same footing with academic subjects. They will be regulated and financed in the same way as are mathematics, physics, English, and the social studies. All children are expected to participate but under regulations which include medical supervision, health examinations, and the equalization of competing groups. Participation in athletics will not depend on marks in academic subjects. On the other hand, competitions will be limited in such a way as to discourage the exploitation of players for gate receipts, and to encourage sports for their own sake and the sake of the individual. The program is designed to promote general health and to prevent mental, physical, and social handicaps in young persons."

While the success of this program depends in large measure on the extent to which local boards of education accept the regulations of the State Regents, and on the manner in which local communities finance the plan, it is a tremendous step forward. Here is the very foundation for character and morals, even for the "higher morality," for emotional poise, for practical rather than theoretical sex education, for lessons in coöperation and sportsmanship, for the understanding of citizenship, for the effective personality in any democratic social order.

"I got ninety in my physical education quiz," a twelve-year-old girl announced one day. "What do you mean by physical education quiz?" her mother asked. "How can you have a paper test in physical education?" Whereupon the daughter explained that there were twenty questions on the rules and techniques of tennis, reviewing what they had been taught on the playing field.

We can teach the rules in tennis, but in the fields of marriage, economics, local and national government, and the various phases of personality, our educational sys-

tem believes in teaching children to work out their own
codes. Our civilization has not yet accepted the most
elementary codes or axioms in these important fields.

NO BUSINESS WITHOUT CODES

The one conspicuous activity in which our civilization has developed the rules of the game, other than the
field of competitive sports and the fields of science, is
business. Almost any person, including myself, can point
out many faults in business. Its faults have been made
obvious, its virtues have been obscured.

The elementary fact about the structure of large and
small business enterprises, including agriculture, is this:
Business carries the entire burden of education, of
local and national government, art and music, public improvements, life insurance, welfare agencies of all kinds,
social security, the army and navy, etc. Such business
would never have been possible without a highly developed code of morals and practices. The policy in stores
of having only one price on merchandise, instead of
cryptic letters subject to personal interpretation by the
seller, was a great advance in the honesty and economy
of business. The credit system which makes it possible
to sell and ship or buy and receive goods to and from all
ends of the world is a triumph in the creation of rules.
These credit transactions represent an infinitely complex
code of honesty and keeping promises, with a minimum
of misunderstanding and friction. The certainty with
which employees receive an agreed-on piece-work or
weekly wage, the confidence with which people buy

articles of an advertised quality, the reliable systems of delivery, the liberality in accepting returns, and an infinite number of other details represent the highly developed rules of business conduct.

Only through the development of these many clean-cut rules and techniques has business been able to support the fast-growing burden of government and education. These rules, like the rules in competitive sports, have made it possible to substitute work for haggling, action for debate, coöperation for competitive quarrels.

We hear much about the ruinous competition in business. The epic fact about business is its marvelous coöperation, between businesses themselves, between business and the public, and between employers and employees. Business represents teamwork of a superlative order, an activity which has developed most of its rules through its own progressive thinking.

The material advances of civilization and the standard of physical living have been attributed usually to technological developments. Inventions, science, machinery, have been given the credit. We are beginning to realize, and we shall see with painful clarity as present social trends continue, that technological advances are useless in comparison with the development of codes and techniques for coöperation in business.

The failure of business to provide employment for many people is due, in my opinion, not to technological unemployment but to artificial interruptions in the evolution of business codes especially by government. To be sure, business men have often invited governmental subsidies and therefore governmental control. However, in revising the rules of football, experts experienced in the game are elected to the rules committee. In the field of business, political boards and appointees who have never mastered the elementary rules of business, increasingly make its rules. The inevitable result is havoc and growing unemployment. Moreover, government has also gone into actual competition with business. This is as though the umpire were to pick up the ball, blow the whistle, run for a touchdown, and declare himself the winner.

CHILDREN OF INDUSTRIAL DIVORCE

An example of governmental interruption is the arbitrary creation, virtually by law, of labor unions. Labor unions may be desirable, but their sudden and artificial promotion creates more problems than it solves. It resembles the sudden assembling of many teams without adequate traditions or codes. Such teams, arbitrarily introduced at the Olympic Games, would result in chaos. Introduced in business they have had the same effect. The encouragement of labor unions by government solves no problems, it only creates them. For when a labor union has been duly certified, the problem of developing teamwork between employers and employees still remains and will continue to remain.

In this respect, labor legislation in the United States has been much like the laws of divorce. Their emphasis is on breaking up the game rather than on preserving it. The English labor laws are framed to prevent quarrels between employers and employees at the expense of the public. They subordinate the selfish impulses of all classes to the general good. They codify the principle of good sportsmanship in industry. Our laws do exactly the contrary. They codify hatred and distrust, and they breed these emotions among employers and employees at large. Above all, they disregard the rights and welfare of the public. A few hundred men may throw ten thousand out of work and upset a whole city. In America, the public becomes the children of industrial divorce.

DEMOCRACY AND ITS UMPIRE

Democracy is the conspicuous expression of the ideals of sportsmanship in government. The essence of democracy is a constitution or body of laws to which people *voluntarily* subordinate themselves including even their voting powers. Like true sportsmen they say in effect: "We are going to pursue the game of life under these rules, and these rules are more important than winning the game. They are more important than any one man or group of men who may want to take a short-cut to the abundant life by side-stepping the Constitution. If I do not win as often under these rules as do certain other people, I will do what any good sportsman does, namely, learn from my mistakes and the success of others, and practice all the harder."

And yet, though this is democracy, the rules of football have been more systematically cherished and brought up-to-date than have the laws of the Constitution of the United States. For the laborious task of developing the Constitution, we have substituted the methods of hasty legislation and the concept of a liberal Supreme Court. In competitive sports, the umpires have no license to interpret the rules liberally, they must interpret them literally. If this process works injustice, then the rules are carefully amended. The intellectual arrogance of our time, however, has created the tradition of liberalism in the Supreme Court. That is to say, justices assume the right to interpret the Constitution, not according to what it says, but liberally, in accordance with the times. Consequently, the interpretations have changed with individual justices while the laws have remained largely static.

A Supreme Court which establishes the principle of interpreting the Constitution liberally is bound to encourage the demand for a set of judges who will be still more liberal in their interpretations. This demand will crystallize through men whose greed for power makes them impatient with the slow processes of democracy. Such men will take courage from a public which no longer understands or respects democracy, a public which is anxious to take short-cuts to the abundant life, a public educated in the belief that the end justifies the means, a public which has lost its ideals of good sportsmanship.

This is the inevitable result of a liberalism which substitutes the easy path of interpreting the rules for the more difficult process of improving the rules. And this is the road to a government by temperamental men rather than a government by impersonal laws, a dictatorship in place of a constitutional democracy.

A HIGHER UMPIRE

Religion, like democracy, involves the voluntary submission of the individual to a code of morals which he puts above his personal interests. These morals of right and wrong are the supreme rules of sportsmanship in every phase of life. The concept of God is that of a supreme Umpire whose decisions have an authority beyond that of any human being. Even though anthropomorphic, this concept represents a faith in the experience of the human race and the precepts it has developed through countless generations. It attributes an authority and wisdom to these rules far above the private wisdom of any one man or group of men in the present.

However, our civilization, far from accepting the precepts of the race as embodied in religion, has steadily repudiated their authority. The Ten Commandments, for example, even though accepted in theory, have been interpreted with a liberalism which has rendered them almost meaningless in social practice. Some leaders of the Church, the custodian of religion and morals, have contributed to this process. Instead of developing the codes of religion, as we develop the rules in sports, so that they apply with increasing definiteness to the modern complexities of life, to marriage and the family, to the morals of government, to character and personality, they have followed the general intellectual trend toward liberal interpretations and vagueness.

TOWARD A NEW AND BETTER WORLD

A better civilization will surely develop these codes. It will firmly attach itself to the religious experience of the human race and, with intellectual humility, build its structure on this foundation. Unlike our society, which tests the old by the new, this society will test the new by the old.

In the field of competitive sports, rules are evolved to improve the sport, to remove unfair practices, to give every player a more equal chance. However, the rules are always the same for every player. Each competitor is judged by the same standards and given the same opportunities. The player or the team which wins is congratulated by the losers, and the losers blame themselves and not the winners or the rules for their failure. They have made the effort which in itself has been supremely worthwhile, and if winning is so important, they are still free to practice and try further. This is sportsmanship. This is the path to personality.

Unquestionably, the laws of government could be improved to give every citizen a more equal chance. In our civilization, however, and in the United States especially, the professional law-makers and politicians have rushed to pass laws which make the chances more unequal. There is one set of rules for the farmers, another set for labor unions, another set for the employers, another for the rich, another for the poor, etc. In actual operation, these laws mean that the laborer pays taxes or higher food prices to help the poor farmer, and the farmer pays higher prices for machinery and materials to raise the wages of the poor laborer. Therefore both remain poor. In fact, both are bound to become poorer still because of the waste motion and bickering involved. They are like two teams each playing according to its own rules. Whichever wins at the moment, both will lose in the end.

Yet these are the rules which our civilization has come to crave, rules which will give each group some special advantage in the game. Many people no longer want equal opportunities or rules that are the same for all individuals and classes; they want special rules that will guarantee their winning in advance. They want favors and favoritism. They have become defeatists. They blame their failures on the successful, on old-fashioned laws, on anything but themselves.

Even the fairest rules do not create personality or character. Only the acceptance of those rules by the individual and his efforts under them develop the habits and skills of competence. Unequal rules and the rules of favoritism will not convert weak personalities into strong ones. Their result will be to make the weak weaker still and at the same time to ruin the strong who now make it possible for the weak to survive.

Moreover, the passing of new laws to provide unequal rules for special groups quickly produces a disregard for all laws. The liberal interpretation of basic laws, to hasten social justice as demanded by first one group and then another, inevitably creates a disrespect for the whole concept of law. A liberal interpretation in one situation breeds a still more liberal one in another and the end is complete liberalism, that is, perfect anarchy in which every individual and group makes its own laws.

Sit-down strikes, mutinies on board ship, lawless pick-eting, coercion of workers by violence, breaking of contracts, unlawful strikes, are symptoms of the cur-rent trend. The ominous fact is the attitude of officials and judges who fail to apply the existing laws to these acts, and to discipline their perpetrators in the manner clearly prescribed. Some are moral and political cowards, others are sincere if mistaken liberals, who believe that the purpose of the law-breakers justifies their means. In either case, a still further disregard for the laws is in-vited. This tendency toward anarchy has made tre-mendous headway in the past few years, hindered at times by a few old-fashioned thinkers, but accelerated by many of the great intellectual liberals in power.

Ironically, this concept of liberalism, namely that the ends of social justice are more important than the meth-ods for their achievement, emanates not from the igno-rant but from the educated. It has taken the hopeful products of our great educational system to develop the practice of modern liberalism, or, as will become increas-ingly obvious, the techniques leading to anarchism.

The psychology of personality and of its development remains the same, whether it be in the simpler or the more complicated situations of life, in the kindergarten or in government. Its essence is sportsmanship; that is putting the rules of the game above personal passions and reason, the game itself above personal victory. There can be no short-cuts to personality, either in competitive sports or in the other games of life. The person who tries to interpret or change the rules to suit himself or his friends, only injures the personalities involved. He creates long-drawn-out arguments and quarrels which interrupt the game, thus blocking the energies, slowing the process of learning, and converting coöperative competition into competitive chaos.

I visualize a civilization which recognizes the potentialities of the individual, and whose social measures are designed to help rather than hinder the development of personality.

In such a civilization sportsmanship will not be confined to the athletic field but will be embodied in every phase of life, the classroom, the family, the community, the nation. This civilization will make competitive sports the very foundation of its educational system, because here the lessons of sportsmanship, of impersonal disciplines, of social coöperation, of energetic competition, in short, of personality, are so effectively learned.

It will include, in its education, universal work projects of economic value, in which the disciplines of business will be sharply reproduced, so as to develop the habits of economic self-determination so stifled by our present education. In place of summer vacations for children from ten to eighteen, there will be summer camps or farms which will be just as essential a part of education as that which we now have, and for all children rich and poor.

It will bend its efforts to developing codes of sportsmanship in respect to marriage, in respect to civic affairs, in respect to democracy and government. The codes of sex, marriage, local and national citizenship will be universally taught. Far more time and care will be given to these matters than is the case today. They will be taught as are arithmetic or the rules of tennis, that is, as facts rather than as theories, as moral obligations rather than as privileges, in short, as indispensable parts of personality and good citizenship.

This civilization will have less regimentation in non-essentials and more in the essentials. Competitive sports will be among the essentials in every year, but in forms adjusted to the physique of the individual. Algebra, geometry, and the foreign languages will be among the non-essentials, except in courses which require such subjects for practical reasons. The Ten Commandments, the Constitution of the United States, Lincoln's Gettysburg Address, and many other significant documents will have to be learned and understood so far as individual comprehension permits.

Reading, writing, and arithmetic are habits which must be universally taught because they represent the means of communication between people. The same should be true of the basic habits and codes of personality. However, beyond the grade school level there should be less regimentation and more consideration for individuality and vocational superiority. Instead of eight years of the wrong kind of regimentation in high school and college, as now so often happens, each child will have an eight-hour examination or more by a competent psychologist, to help guide the parents and child in the selection of a program befitting his aptitudes. These examinations will be given before choosing a high school course, and again before choosing a college course, at public centers not connected with any one school.

Pupils will emerge with the fundamental habits of personality already acquired, the basic habits of playing and working with others. They will not have to waste their adult life in trying to discover what personality and happiness are. Having learned the codes and many of the habits, their minds will be released for the constructive aspects of living, for the development of a socially creative individuality.

Only a civilization which appreciates the values and principles of personality generally can put such a program into effect. From a scientific point of view, psychology is rapidly demonstrating the basic principles and techniques. It has already shown that personality depends upon releasing a person's mind from preoccupation with himself and with the general theories of living by training him in the actual habits of social living from an early age on. The more complete codification of these habits and their institutional expression will be the great contribution of the new civilization to the progress of the race. Just as our civilization has codified the habits of science and given man control over his physical environment, so the next step will give man greater control over himself and his social institutions.

IX

GOLD STANDARDS OF
PERSONALITY

IX

GOLD STANDARDS OF
PERSONALITY

IF I WERE to say that the purpose of education should
be to teach people, not how to think, but how to
avoid thinking, many would throw up their hands in
horror. One of the sacred cows of education is this belief that the primary function of education is to teach
people to think for themselves. From the standpoint of
the psychology of the mind and its development, there
could be no more damaging belief than this.

*If organized education does not increasingly teach
people how to avoid unnecessary thinking, then there is
no excuse for its existence.*

The experience of the race has given man many valuable lessons of right and wrong. If these lessons were
properly summed up and taught by the forces of education, individuals would be saved a great deal of unnecessary thinking. However, education emphasizes the importance of having each individual think out his own
standards and so create, in one lifetime, what it has taken
thousands of generations and millions of thinkers to produce. This process I describe as the *egocentric morbidity*

of education. Progressive education represents a whole philosophy built around this theory. Self-expression and original thinking are emphasized at the expense of the disciplines and principles developed by the past. The current philosophy that we are in a new and rapidly changing social order in which the old must be tested by the new, is based on this morbidly egocentric point of view.

Another dogma of education is that knowledge is power. Today it is quite evident that knowledge may be a source of confusion and weakness. Intellectual Polly-annas have preached with increasing fervor the importance of educating a nation in economics, government, international relations, democracy, etc. Now that people know infinitely more about these subjects than before, they seem farther away from the truth than ever.

"Life is becoming more and more complicated. Its intricacies threaten the very sanity of people." How often we hear statements like this. And yet, the complexities of life are largely matters of each person's own making. To one person life is comparatively simple and well within his powers. To another, living in exactly the same environment, life is baffling and beyond his grasp.

In these days, to describe a person as a man of ideas is to praise him, as a man of principles is virtually to condemn him. And yet, ideas and knowledge without basic principles can lead only to conflict and impotence. The great value of principles or standards is that they enable a person to meet the complexities and contradictions of life with a minimum of wasteful thinking. When an idea occurs to him or is pressed upon him, he can accept or reject it quickly. The person without adequate principles is like one without exact standards of truth. He is caught in a web of ideas which he must evaluate in terms of expediency. One expedient leads to another, like the progressive expedients of a lie, and the result is personal and social discord.

The chief need of individuals and society today is the codification of standards and principles in order that the present terrific waste of energies and ruinous thinking may be reduced. The term *gold standards* is used here merely as an apt analogy. The abandoning of the gold standard is a conspicuous example of the current trend toward substituting a yardstick in somebody's mind for a yardstick which is relatively fixed.

THE PSYCHOLOGY OF GOLD

Gold is a psychological device or yardstick to help people and nations make and keep certain promises.* Gold has never been a perfect yardstick but it has been one of the most nearly fixed and uniform articles known to man. For this reason it was chosen as the basis of money. When a man made a purchase or obtained a loan, he could agree with the second party to pay a certain amount in gold or paper dollars redeemable in gold. However, the value of gold in terms of the goods which

* Since this was written there has appeared a great book, *The Promises Men Live By,* Harry Sherman, Random House, 1938. This book promises to revolutionize the sterile subject of economics. It does exactly what we have been discussing, resolves a confusion of facts and fallacies through basic principles and values of human nature.

it would buy changed considerably from time to time. Therefore, when a man paid the amount of gold agreed on, he might at one time lose by the transaction, and at another time gain by it. Nevertheless, so long as the gold standard stood, it was gold he had to pay, and gold which his creditor had to accept. About this there was no confusion or arguing, no question of expediency, whoever stood to lose by the bargain. Individuals or nations might, in unusual circumstances, agree to adjust some injustice due to unexpected circumstances. However, this agreement would still be in terms of gold. The contract might be changed but the standard would still be gold.

Thus, by adhering to the gold standard, which was relatively definite, individuals and nations were able to make and to keep promises with a minimum of discussion and disagreement. The great business and trade of the world were developed with a minimum of friction and misunderstanding. The World War, however, brought about a destruction in values and ideals which made it extremely difficult for certain nations to pay their debts in gold. Therefore, instead of debtors and creditors striving their best to arrive at new and more practical agreements, one nation after another decided to abandon the gold standard.

In its place has been substituted what is called a *managed currency* or managed money. In the United States this means that certain government officials have the power to say that a paper dollar shall be worth eighty cents in gold, or sixty, or fifty, as may in their wisdom seem best. The value of money, therefore, resides entirely in the minds of the men who control it. As a result of their thoughts the dollar may be worth more or less than it is now.

Therefore, when individuals are considering large business transactions, they can no longer estimate their costs or loans by a gold standard; they can only speculate on what the managers of money will decide. If business men wish to make an agreement involving the payment of certain sums of money, that agreement must be subjected to the changes in the value of money which its managers might decree. If a person wishes to take out a life insurance policy or save a certain part of his income through a savings account, what the amounts will be worth a few years hence also depends on what goes on in the minds of the currency managers.

In short, instead of an impersonal gold standard which until 1914 automatically reflected the mistakes and sins of individuals and nations, we have a personally managed standard of money. This personal management is bound to reflect the prejudices and passions, the ignorance and wisdom, of the few who manage. The situation is very much like that of a family in which the parents have no impersonal or gold standards of conduct. The children never know where they stand or what to expect. The result is uncertainty and fear.

So in a nation or in a collection of nations, the substitution of personal minds and their personal money standards for an impersonal gold standard, creates indecision and suspense. People accustomed to making and keeping promises now hesitate, because they cannot rely on the decisions of the money managers. This uncer-

tainty is far greater than any of those ever created by
the gold standard. There is endless speculation and talk
about the plans of the managers; uncertainty is made
more certain, and the production of goods which gives
money its real value is curtailed. As in the case of personality, the substitution of a personal standard for an
impersonal standard inevitably results in the disintegration of will-power, in this case the will-power of millions.

The silver dollar still bears this inscription: "In God
We Trust." "What god?" we might ask. The god of a
personally managed currency? The god of selfish nation-
alism? The god of expediency for whom the end justifies
the means? The god of the arrogant mind which pre-
sumes to manage millions of people better than they can
manage themselves? Maybe all of these, and any but the
true God.

When our forefathers adopted this inscription they
meant it and it meant something to them. It meant their
acceptance of a standard of values higher than money itself, whether on the gold standard or any other. It meant
their trust in a Wisdom far beyond that of government
officials who would manage a currency. It meant their
trust in the powers of people under this standard to develop their personalities and to create the wealth which
would give value to their dollar.

The gold standard, psychologically, was merely a
useful device for curtailing the vagaries and uncertainties of personally managed currencies. Gold does not
think. It was an impersonal standard for economizing
human energies and releasing them for productive work.
Our forefathers saw what all the theories and long-

winded discussions of economists have failed to clarify, namely: the stability and value of any currency is no greater than the stability and character of the people behind that currency.

Because people generally, in sacrificing a higher moral order, have lost their own stability and character, they have invited a personally managed currency which adds still further instability and uncertainty. This is not to say that there can be no stability without a return to the old gold standard. It does mean that there can be no development of stability until some impersonal standard of money is devised. That is to say, there must be standards of honesty and character, so that people's promises do not mean one thing today and something different a year hence.

WILL-POWER

How strong is a person's will? What is will-power? Is it a subconscious force of unknown quantity? Is it something that can be developed, and if so how? These questions go to the heart of the problem of personality. Every person dissatisfied with himself or striving to achieve a better life asks himself these questions in some form or other. Can I be the master of my fate, within what limits, and how?

One of the traits in the P.Q. or Personality Quotient test is that called self-determination. This trait is measured by the extent to which the individual has acquired habits of doing the things he knows he should do rather than the things he merely feels like doing, things which are right rather than things which are always pleasant. For example, the child may acquire the habit of doing his homework first and listening to the radio afterwards, of practicing the piano when he would rather be reading a story book, of going to a Scout meeting when he would rather be seeing a motion picture, of telling the uncomfortable truth when an evasion would be so much more pleasant. Hundreds of specific habits like these are acquired by the child only under discipline. They represent activities and standards which the parents or society consider desirable and which they enforce regardless of the child's desires, impulses or arguments. When the child has acquired these habits he has also acquired the standards or ideals they represent.

This, psychologically, is the origin of will-power. Having been determined by his parents up to a point, but not too far, the child gains the power to determine himself. He has developed a collection of activities and standards which he values above his personal impulses, and a momentum of habits and skills which enables him to do those things which are desirable rather than those which are merely pleasant.

Often when we are dealing with young people or adults whose personalities and will-power are weak, their history compels us to talk to them somewhat as follows: "Your basic difficulty is that you have always relied too heavily on your own judgment. You have been governed by the principle of doing as you pleased or thought best. Possibly your parents, in your early childhood, permitted you far too much freedom in having your own way. You developed a will of your own. You became self-willed. The more you had your own way the more you took it. Therefore, instead of learning to do a great many things which would have been good for your development, you did only those things which you wanted to do. Instead of learning to do the things which other people and the world consider desirable, you did only those which you judged desirable.

"Now that you realize that something must be done, you are beset by a sense of inferiority. You are doubtful about your will-power to do even the things you want to do. You are confused and uncertain both about what you want to do and about what you ought to do. Our personality tests reflect this state in that they rate you below average in habits of self-sufficiency or making your own decisions. By developing a personal standard of living in accord with your own ideas, you have developed chaos rather than certainty. Your personally managed standard of action has deteriorated into an unmanageable collection of conflicts.

"The remedy for this situation is to adopt some definite goal and program of action such as we may now agree on. This goal and this program may not be easy. Much of it may run counter to your inclinations and personal impulses. However, as soon as you have definitely adopted it, many of your decisions will be automatically simplified and made easier. You will be like a traveler with a destination in mind. The road may not be perfectly clear, but when tempting by-ways or distractions present themselves, you will at least have some standard by which to recognize them and reject them.

"This program, once adopted, must become for you

a gold standard of thinking and acting. That is, instead of wasting your thoughts on how to avoid it or make it easier, you will learn to take it for granted and concentrate your energies on carrying it into action. Your present weak will-power is due to your excessive planning to adjust the world to suit your personal desires. The more you planned to suit yourself, the more confused you became. Now you will stop trying to adjust the plan to yourself and adjust yourself to the plan instead. The sportsman, instead of wasting his energies arguing about the rules of the game, concentrates his energies on playing the game. So you, instead of thinking and worrying about whether this program is practical or pleasant, will economize your energies for its execution."

This is the psychology of will-power and its development. The will must have objectives and standards on which to fasten itself. When the proper standards have not been developed in childhood or youth, then an artificial decision like that just described becomes necessary. In such a decision the tremendous resources of human nature are dramatically revealed. Here we see individuals rising to great heights. Here we see them call on an inner strength representing sheer will. The psychologist who refuses to become a wet-nurse to his clients often sees this phenomenon. It is, of course, the basic phenomenon in religion, where the individual is born again by subordinating his personally managed morality to the gold standard of a higher order.

No individual is capable of many supreme decisions or calls upon sheer will-power. However, if a wise decision is made, the detailed mechanics or habits for its execution are more likely to be developed. The level of his capacity for future decisions will be raised. Even in a simple matter like a child's deciding to do his homework in short division instead of having a good time, this decision makes him more capable of doing long division, etc. The son, who decides to give up an allowance from his parents and to embark on a less comfortable plan of action, is on the way toward developing habits of self-reliance and economic independence.

The weak will-power of adults, we find, can often be attributed to one of three causes. Their parents either allowed them as children to have their own way too much. Or they imposed their own will on them too completely or for too long a time. Or they possessed no adequate set of standards or ideals themselves and therefore lacked any consistent plan of discipline for their children. The first two causes really arise from the third. Only an impersonal standard followed by the parents and applied impartially can avoid the excesses of too little discipline or of parental possessiveness. The standards of personality are gold standards, and must be treated as such. They are not matters which either parents or children can tamper with to suit their personal ends. Every attempt to change these rules in the middle of the game, to reason out a pleasant evasion, creates confusion and weakens the will of both parents and children.

Firm but impersonal standards of discipline, applied by parents or teachers consistently, create in children a profound feeling of security. They know where they stand, what they may do, and what to expect. They are saved the exhausting hysterics of emotional arguments.

Obedience, they know, comes first and reasoning about the wisdom of a particular rule is secondary. Having obeyed a rule they often learn to understand it infinitely better than they would through days of so-called reasoning. Knowing the certainty of their parents or teachers, children develop a certainty of their own. Within this framework of certainty they concentrate their energies on the development of competence. Their energies are freed to do the desirable things rather than bound to argue about their desirability. Through respecting an impersonal authority they acquire authority over themselves. They are on the way to becoming the captains of their souls.

PSYCHOLOGICAL TESTS

In examining young people with the aid of tests, we are often impressed with the peculiar character of their responses. In the beginning a person may be quite skeptical and reticent. We make very little effort to penetrate his reserves or to make him talk. Instead, we proceed to ask him a series of matter-of-fact questions about his personal history. How many brothers and sisters has he, are his parents living, what has been his education, his favorite subjects, the subjects he liked least, his outdoor and indoor amusements, etc. The procedure seems almost like the routine of filling out a questionnaire for an insurance policy, and yet many of the facts asked for are quite personal. For example, how did he spend his time yesterday evening, and the evening before that, and so on for a week. None of the questions call for much discussion, most of them refer to the person's past and present activities. We are not interested so much in what he thinks as in what he has done, and when we know what he has done, we already have many clues to what he will think when he begins to talk freely.

On the basis of the facts thus obtained, we select, from the hundreds of available tests, those most suitable to this particular problem. If a vocational problem is involved possibly eight or more are selected, and we start the person on these tests with some such remark as: "Before talking with you more freely, we wish to have you do a few things which will give us certain cross-sections of your habits, interests, and aptitudes." For six, possibly ten or twelve hours, the person is fully occupied with these tests. When the completed battery of tests has been graded by an assistant, the results are studied by the examining psychologist in preparation for the coming interview.

The individual, by this time, is in a considerable state of suspense, wondering what the results will be, often expecting the worst. Therefore the psychologist immediately begins to give him the facts, possibly as follows: "In the Otis test of scholastic capacity, sometimes called general intelligence, you excelled 85% of high school seniors (students) and 68% of college students. That is, your performance was superior to that of 68% of the college freshmen, sophomores, juniors and seniors in twenty-one colleges on whom this test was standardized. In the Iowa test of the mechanics of English, that is, spelling and grammar, you excelled 85% of the 14,000 entering college freshmen on whom this test was stand-

ardized. However, in the Iowa test of mathematics aptitude, you excelled only 27% of entering college freshmen, and in the O'Rourke test of mechanical aptitude,
you excelled only 19% of the 9,000 young men on
whom Dr. O'Rourke standardized his test. Evidently
your mechanical and mathematical aptitudes are not
such as to suggest an engineering course or profession,"
etc.

The impression made by such a collection of facts is
usually terrific. The reasons for this impression are obvious. The person being examined sees clearly that he is
receiving the quite impersonal results of a set of standardized tests, and not the personal opinions of the
examiner. He is not being told a flattering story about
himself but being given a cold-blooded comparison between himself and thousands of other people in respect
to certain points. Some of the comparisons may please
his ego, others may be quite unpleasant; nevertheless he
accepts both as equally true. The personality of the
examining psychologist is, in this situation, quite subordinate to the objective facts revealed by these highly
standardized tests. These standards, he sees, definitely
limit the interpretations which the psychologist can
make, and this adds to his confidence in the psychologist's final conclusions.

In short, the individual acquires confidence not in the
psychologist as such, but rather in the impersonal techniques and standards developed by the science of psychology. This confidence gives a powerful impetus to
his decisions and a solid foundation for his program of
action. When the individual knows where he stands,

both in respect to his strength and weakness, he can economize his energies to greatest advantage. This, of itself, is a source of greater power.

PROGRESSIVE STANDARDS

We may contrast the psychological procedure with a theory and practice which is being rapidly applied in the schools and which is one of the basic tenets of progressive education. The gist of this theory is that rigid marking systems should be abolished because their use gives backward children a sense of inferiority and able children a sense of superiority. A pupil who gets marks of thirty and fifty in spelling and arithmetic tests, for example, while others get marks of eighty and ninety, is likely to develop a sense of inferiority which may permanently retard his development. Quite possibly the child is working hard and, considering his natural abilities, is doing good work. Therefore, instead of giving him a numerical mark, or an F (failing) rating, his work should be reported somewhat as follows:

Achievement and Effort: John's attitude is excellent and he is eager to learn. His tests and reviews do not reflect the care shown in his daily work.
Work Habits: His work habits are good. He can be relied on to carry out directions and he coöperates with the other pupils in their work.

Such a report, it is claimed, will not hurt the child's feelings or discourage him in his future efforts.

The further logic underlying this theory is that a pupil's work should be marked, not by a common standard which is the same for all children, but according to his own abilities. "There is only one proper standard for each child and that is," says a leader in progressive education, "is he doing the best of which he is capable?" A group of educators in a large public school system state this theory as follows: "Since we revise the curriculum and our methods to fit the needs and abilities of the individual, we must also change our marking system to harmonize with this principle. *Each pupil should be judged by his own pattern.*"

This theory sounds plausible, especially since it is usually expressed in terms of the emotional idealism so popular today. This idealism may be summed up in a sentence: The welfare of the individual student is more important than any collective or regimented marking system. But what, actually, does this theory involve? It involves the complete abandonment of the concept of honesty and truth as a social institution. Instead of telling John the truth about his work in arithmetic, in marks that John, his parents, or anyone else can understand, the teacher now puts the truth in a manner that neither John, his parents, nor the teacher herself can understand or explain clearly. The teacher marks not by an objective standard of truth but by her own personal standard. That is, she marks John not according to his actual results but according to her interpretation of John's capacities and efforts. Thus she shields John from the objective truth, she conceals the true facts from the parents, and she herself assumes the entire responsibility for her pupils' progress.

The numerical system of marking is by no means perfect, but at least it represents an attempt to substitute objective standards for the subjective vagaries of teachers who are as human as most other people. Progressive education, however, would make each teacher a personal god of truth, creating a standard peculiar to each individual pupil. The truth is to be tempered according to the welfare of the pupil, *as each teacher conceives that welfare*. Only that is true which, in her subjective opinion, is for the pupil's good. And so we find the theory that the end justifies the means as a basic philosophy and technique in progressive education. We begin even in the grade schools to teach and to practice that honesty is a matter of policy rather than a matter of principle, and that objective facts or impersonal standards should be subordinated to personal judgments of what is good for people.

Professor W. E. Hocking, my teacher in ethics, used to say that it was certainly desirable to tell the truth in the most tactful and constructive way possible, but that no individual had the right to put himself between another person and the literal truth. He defined truth as a matter of social morality, not a matter of personal expediency. The teacher who marks a person on the basis of expediency, no matter how noble her object, is assuming a tremendous personal responsibility. Psychologically, she is contributing directly to the pupil's inferiority by protecting him from the real facts, and by keeping him from facing the realities. Inferiority, as we have seen, grows out of a failure to face reality or the facts of life. No wonder so many of our pupils enter the world—as lamented by one of the new texts on progressive education—unprepared for the shocks of life. Here they will not be marked or rewarded on the basis of their capacities and good intentions, but on the basis of what they actually contribute in comparison with others. Even in a communistic system, this fact is fundamental.

Truly, we are rapidly substituting a managed currency of truth for a gold standard of truth in our educational system, and personalities will suffer accordingly.

MENTAL TELEPATHY

Many people have asked what I, as a psychologist, think of mental telepathy. The question has always troubled me for two reasons. In the first place, I am scientifically suspicious of claims made by people who are obviously trying to prove a point. The emotional desires of people can lead them, unconsciously, to do almost anything with evidence to make it prove what they wish to believe. My inclination, therefore, is to wait until their evidence has been tested by less prejudiced investigators. Secondly, the revelations made have usually been so trivial or so concerned with personal details that they had little value to any but the persons immediately involved. I could not become excited over communications which might just as well have been made by a telephone call or a telegram.

When the experiments with cards, conducted at Duke

University by a biologist, Dr. Rhine, led to claims for the proof of an extra sense, called extra-sensory perception, the requests for my opinion multiplied. Aside from the fact that the scientific claims for the soundness of this experiment were first presented by a professor of English, and that many psychologists were already questioning Dr. Rhine's methods and statistics, the answer I had been groping for came to me quite by accident.*

A young woman of my acquaintance was relating to a group of friends an experience with mental telepathy which she had had while in Europe. She was in Paris and had planned, the following day, to leave for a visit in Spain. That night, after going to bed, she heard her mother in Ohio say clearly: "Mary, do not go to Spain! Mary, do not go to Spain." The message was so clear and impressive that, upon waking the next morning, she decided to postpone her trip. A few days later she saw in the papers that the Spanish revolution had broken out and with particular violence in the city to which she was bound. After her return home, she found that her mother, on the day she had received her telepathic message, had been on the point of sending her a warning by cablegram. She had thought the message, but for some reason failed to dispatch it.

The humorous aspect of this incident suddenly came over me. I had heard this mother tell Mary to do things a hundred different times, at a distance of no more than ten feet, and Mary had totally failed to hear her. Evi-

* One of the most complete of the many exposures of the apparent fallacies in the methods and statistics of the "Duke Experiment" may be found in *Scientific Monthly*, October, 1937, by Dr. C. E. Kellogg, professor of psychology at McGill University, Montreal.

dently, it seemed to me then, if parents really want their children to hear and obey them, they should go three thousand miles off and try a message by mental telepathy.

Other incidents then also occurred to me. For example, the player in a bridge game, intensely concentrating his mind on the wish that his partner will lead a certain suit. Yet, though he has already told his partner by his first discard or his opening lead what that suit should be, the partner after laborious thought leads the wrong card! Or the wife who hopes strenuously that her husband will remember to mail the letter she gave him that morning, only to have him arrive home with it in his pocket. Or the teacher who carefully goes over a certain passage with her pupils, only to find that half of them have not even heard her.

It would seem as though to learn how to use the senses we already have is more important than adding a sixth sense to the collection. Mental telepathy and extra-sensory messages would be a gratuitous addition to the present sources of bewilderment and uncertainty. If minds will not listen to or cannot grasp the obvious, how can they evaluate the less obvious?

Therefore it seems to me that mental telepathy merely introduces another variable into the accepted methods of learning which we already have. If we cannot arrive at common standards of thinking and behavior with the present methods, the variable of mental telepathy puts this goal still farther out of reach.

What we have to communicate to each other is infinitely more important than the method by which we commune.

TALK, TALK, TALK

A couple who had married late in life brought us the following problem: The husband was devoted to a semi-invalid mother who had sacrificed her life and energies to the support of a weak husband and three children. She had managed to give all the children a good education, but two of them were now dead and the husband had also died. This son survived, was moderately successful, and had built a home for his mother and himself. To this home he had brought his wife.

After living there several months, the wife found it impossible to go on. Undoubtedly the circumstances were almost impossible, since the mother simply could not give up her possessiveness over her son, nor refrain from managing her daughter-in-law as well. The two women were absolutely at odds. Therefore, the wife took an apartment of her own, which pleased neither the husband, his mother, nor even the wife. The issue between the husband and wife therefore became the disposition of the mother. The husband would not give her up and his wife would not live with her. After weeks of discussion and argument they were no nearer a solution, and so brought the problem to us.

It was perfectly obvious that this man's loyalty to his mother was not a mere emotional involvement, a psychoanalytic mother fixation, but a loyalty growing from a deep sense of duty in keeping with a strong character. Even if we could persuade him to put his mother in a home, his sense of duty and justice would be so violated that, in the end, he would hate his wife as the cause.

Neither could we urge the wife to return to this house under the existing circumstances. They were beyond the fortitude of any but the strongest individual. Therefore we advised them somewhat as follows:

"This is a situation which no one can solve by logic or discussion. We may reason the pros and cons forever without arriving one step nearer a happy compromise. Here the interests of three individuals are basically different. It is the classic triangle of conflicting loves and hatreds. There is not enough love to go around and too much hatred to subdue. The only answer to this problem is to add more love to the total situation, and the only way to do this is by having or adopting a baby."

"But, if we do this," objected the woman, "she will boss both me and the child, and probably ruin the child!"

"Let her try," we suggested. "You owe her a child, and whether she ruins it is an open question. If she loves the child, she will love you more and her son less. Her lonely, shrinking life will once more expand, as will yours and your husband's. All three of you will become more tolerant and unselfish, and while the frictions will be many, the power to bear them and make adjustments will be so much greater. Instead of having only yourselves to think and worry about, you will have the constructive worry and action of bringing up a child."

What happened in this situation is happening in the world at large. Families, schools, boards of arbitration, educators, government officials, legislators, are trying to resolve conflicting interests and hatreds by talk. The more they talk, the more hatreds they stir up and the

farther they are from any final solution. Even the set-
tlements arrived at are usually compromises and expedients which create many new problems and endless
further discussion. Never in the history of the world has
there been as much talk to so little purpose as exists
today.

Moreover, we have even come to deify talk and discussion as the means of solving all the problems of existence. Our great educators have identified discussion with
democracy. Children and teachers should not only be
free to talk about anything, but organized group discussion of all kinds should be systematically encouraged.
Codes of discipline and school conduct should be
evolved by democratic debate rather than by the scientific studies of the competent. Conventions and movements have been multiplied without end, as sounding
boards for those eager to talk in public. Much of the
daily news consists of reported speeches. The youth of
America, emulating their elders, have organized many
youth movements, the essence of which is controversial
talk about the problems of the world. The radio has
placed a final premium on talk, by enabling interesting
speakers, regardless of their soundness, to talk to millions at once.

The open forum has become the last word in democratic education. Here, it is believed, people of diverse
opinions and beliefs will find a clearing house for their
ideas and from the ensuing conflict arrive at a common
understanding. The National Committee of Adult Civic
Education, whose purpose is "To strengthen the fabric
of democracy," states its case for public forums as fol-

lows: "The complexity of the problems facing modern society has caused many countries to lose their faith in government by the people. The most important question facing America today is whether we can keep that faith by making democracy function efficiently enough to survive in a twentieth century world. The test will be whether the citizens themselves are able to solve the problems confronting them as a nation with a maximum of reason and a minimum of passion; or, whether, bewildered by the questions they are called upon to answer, they will shift their responsibilities to the shoulders of a demagogue. It will be a race between adult civic education and time. The public forum program is the best means so far discovered for keeping democracy in the lead." This is the preamble in support of a Federal bill to authorize the expenditure of over two million dollars, in addition to over six hundred thousand dollars already spent, to establish two or three public forums in every state of the Union.

What a comment this is on the efficacy of our total educational system. Having failed to educate people in the true meaning of democracy during their grade school, high school, and college years, we now propose to turn them loose in public forums, in the hope that their discussions will clarify their understanding of and faith in democracy. Moreover, we plan to do this at the very time when many of the country's popular leaders are consistently repudiating the very essentials of democratic government. The local community discussing and managing its own affairs, which it can know and talk about with some intelligence, is the very cornerstone of democracy. And yet the entire trend of government in the United States has been to deprive local communities of their responsibilities, in relief, in public works, in finance, in education, and to substitute an enforced Federal paternalism. This is only one of many ways in which the principles and responsibilities of democracy are being violated.

Truly, the concept of human nature and personality in high places is tragic in its inconsistencies. People of all kinds are expected, by talk, to reconcile conflicting personal and national interests *in the absence of any generally accepted ideals or standards.*

When even their popular leaders fail to agree on the most elementary rules of the game, we expect them to reduce manufactured complexities to a common agreement. Such discussion, as in the case of the three people described above, is more likely to arouse conflicting passions and to confirm selfish interests. Instead of reducing uncertainty it creates still further bewilderment.

The emphasis of our civilization on public speaking rather than on private thinking is the inevitable result of the scuttling of gold standards of morality and conduct, not so much by the masses as by their intellectual leaders. Deliberately or not, the leaders of thought have substituted for impersonal rules of the game, a managed morality, in which the objectives of the abundant life are considered more important than the means by which they are obtained. A managed morality, like a managed currency, depends upon personal judgments and opinions. No finality, no common agreement, no sportsman-like subordination of argument to action is possible on this basis. Controversy and still more controversy is made inevitable, and the more talk there is, the less coöperation and agreement there will be.

We have already shown that the development of personality requires the subordination of talk and reason to gold standards of thinking and to creative action. These rules, in competitive games at least, are developed and improved by chosen representatives in a fashion consistent with democratic processes; but these representatives are chosen by standards in keeping with the game. They are not necessarily great orators but they have learned to play the game under the rules already there. Our concept of democracy has degenerated into that of a debating society. Its rulers are chosen on the basis of their ability to talk and appeal to the emotions of people rather than for their practical experience and their loyalty to the ideals of sportsmanship. This trend of democracy is only natural among a people whose concept of a good personality is limited to a person who can make a good speech or converse well on many topics.

"Our words are loud, our beliefs are weak," says one of the characters in Miss Millay's *Conversations at Midnight*. This book, incidentally, presents the acme of a talking civilization, a civilization which talks most and to least effect just as its day is ending. The less its certainty, the more it has to say, and the more it emphasizes the importance of talking and of talking well. "To speak well is to speak with authority." More and more people learn to talk with authority, and their authority is "the certain voice of an uncertain moment." In a civilization, as in a person, this is the path to decay, the death of energy and will. Science may continue to repair bodies and to lengthen physical life,

"But how shall the bleeding of the will-to-live be stopped?
What shall we do for gangrene in the mind?"

X

SLAVERY OR PERSONALITY?

X

SLAVERY OR PERSONALITY?

Aᶠᵗᵉʳ centuries of painful progress toward freedom
and democracy, the world is rapidly moving back
into social slavery. Whole nations are submitting themselves to dictatorships and to autocratic governments.
Great populations are giving up their intellectual, economic and moral freedom. The state is becoming supreme and even religion and the churches are made
instruments of the state when they are not actually destroyed.

Such slavery does not just happen. It must be de-
served. Individuals must become the slaves of their own
bad habits before they are ready for the shackles of an
autocratic government. In the United States, which is
moving in the same general direction, we can still observe the process by which people are being prepared.
This process, already described in detail in earlier chapters, is true not only of individuals but of whole populations.

THE STEPS INTO BONDAGE

At its very base are science and education which, bit
by bit, have whittled away the soul of man. For man,

the creator of science and a scientific world, has been substituted the concept of man as the *victim of the very world which he has created*. Man is no longer a free being, a responsible being; he is a cog in a heartless machine, a machine which exists *only in his own mind*. For an idealism based on the values of personality he has substituted an idealism based on the values of a machine. The truly admirable and fruitful disciplines of scientific truth have crowded out the less easily demonstrated moral and spiritual truths. Man is less of a man by his own choice.

Through science mankind has achieved a miraculous power over physical things but at the expense of a decreasing power over itself. Men's bodies now soar through the heavens but their spirits still drag the ground, their bombs bringing devastation to helpless cities.

Through science life has been made physically easier for rich and poor. Hours of work are shorter, the years of free education are longer, conveniences are innumerable, books are to be had for the asking, labor-saving devices are everywhere. In 1900 in the United States there were no radios, one family in seven had a bathtub, and practically none owned automobiles. Today two-thirds or more have bathtubs, almost as many own automobiles, and over eighty percent have radios. The predominating amusements—the radio, movies, and reading—are no longer privileges but universal rights.

As life has become easier, even for the unemployed, character and personality have become weaker. A whole nation suffers from a clogging of the energies and its consequent neuroticisms and fears. As personalities become weaker, they become also more receptive to the promises of politicians who would give them the abundant life for still less effort. The wealthy are already slaves to their possessions. The comparatively poor are rapidly selling their freedom for mere promises of greater abundance.

The social studies have rationalized the growing gap between wishbone and backbone through elaborate schemes for saving man from his own helplessness. The plans for social security, for government housing, for agricultural and labor control, a managed currency, the artificial redistribution of wealth, are plans to do wholesale for people what they are believed unable to do for themselves. All such plans are steps in the enslavement of individuals, even though they voluntarily vote to surrender their responsibilities and freedom to the state. World events have shown that people are seldom aware of the steps leading to economic and governmental serfdom until they have gone too far to retrace their course.

The popular passion for social security through government and law is a dramatic confession of people's growing preference for bondage rather than freedom. Government can give its citizens either freedom or social security, but it cannot give them both. The son who prefers to let his family support him always sacrifices his independence and freedom in the process. Democracy in the United States has meant freedom to all citizens in the pursuit of happiness. To the extent that people now choose security they must sacrifice freedom and opportunity and even democracy itself. Democracy can only succeed with strong, independent people. The decay of character in the United States makes paternalistic dictatorships almost inevitable. Whether this dictatorship be called fascism, communism, or modernized democracy is immaterial.

Now, completing this process of decay is the new liberalism, by which every liberal interprets the rules of life according to his private reason. No longer is liberalism the painful prerogative of the rugged non-conformist; it has become a pleasant process of rationalization for the masses. Everybody's doing it! The liberals in high places interpret the rules for a nation, the lesser liberals interpret the rules of education, the humblest liberal interprets the rules of his personal life. The net result is a nation of individuals preoccupied with avoiding the old rules and making new rules, instead of with playing the game. Every liberal has an ax to grind, which is only human, but every liberal grinds it in his own way, which means confusion. There are as many theories of life today as there are liberals to interpret them. The result is that life itself stops as liberal thinking proceeds.

Liberalism is the final step by which individuals enslave themselves. Where every person insists on thinking for himself, in his own way, all impersonal standards of thinking disappear and thinking itself becomes useless. The very foundations for straight thinking are destroyed. Worse still, the thinking of one person contradicts that of another and the ensuing conflicts generate hate, anger, and even violence. The inevitable result is a dictator who will tell all liberals, high and low, what they may think and what not—at least aloud.

Such are the causes for the decay of personality and the creation of bondage as they are rapidly proceeding in the United States and elsewhere today. Every one of these causes represents a failure to understand the nature of character and personality. Every one of them represents the adoption of ideas and goals which weaken rather than strengthen personality.

Only through a better understanding of personality, through a more complete rediscovery of man, shall we find the keys to our present perplexities. How, for example, do the concepts of personality, advanced thus far, contribute to an understanding of fascism and communism? Fascism and communism represent distinct philosophies of personality quite different from those represented by democracy. These philosophies are no longer abstract and academic subjects. They exist in actual practice around us. They are subjects of continual discussion and debate. Nevertheless the utmost confusion about their meaning persists. Indeed, many people who loudly condemn fascism, for example, have strongly advocated measures which substitute a centralized authority for widely distributed local authorities, the very measures which make fascism or its like inevitable.

PERSONALITY UNDER FASCISM

Every family represents a little fascism of its own. The father or the mother, sometimes both, is the dictator over a family and its children. He makes its laws, he tells the children what to do and what not to do. He governs the family budget. But whereas the purpose of fascism in the family is to develop the personalities of children to the point where they will be wholly independent, state fascism tends to keep its citizens forever dependent. Family fascism is a means of training children in the habits of self-determination. State fascism trains its adults in the habits of perpetual subordination and obedience. The one develops personalities for the freedom and responsibilities of a democracy, ideally speaking. The other disciplines people for the economic and intellectual bondage of perpetual *stateism*.

Under fascism, a dictator may give orders amounting to laws. Since the dictator is supreme, there are no restraints on the laws he can pass. If he decides to raise armies and build battleships, then it must be done. If he decides to raise taxes, taxes will be raised. If he decides to run industry, regulate hours and wages, fix prices, then this program will be executed. If he decides to change the value of money, its value will be changed. If he decides to declare war, then war it is.

Under these uncertainties, the development of personalities is seriously retarded. Since people never know exactly where they stand, they never know quite what to do. It is as though athletes were trying to train for football without being sure of the rules. Of what good would it be to train in forward pass plays when, in the very middle of the season, the officials might decide to abolish forward passes entirely? All business and social enterprise depending on the initiative of individuals or groups is checked for the same reason.

DEMOCRACY—MANY PERSONALITIES

Dictatorship, whether it be called fascism or communism, is a matter of one dominating personality, whereas democracy is a government of many personalities. Instead of one super-personality we have a Constitution which permits many strong personalities, none of whom, however, shall have powers beyond those prescribed. The very strength of a democracy lies in its encouragement of innumerable personalities, in politics, in government, in business, in education, in journalism, etc. When one outstanding personality or group of personalities begins to dominate a country, its constitution and its courts, then democracy is in danger of death.

The constitution of a democracy is a minimum framework of laws under which citizens have agreed to live and let live. Within these laws the individual is free to work out his own destiny. Only the people themselves can change the laws of the constitution. The more stable these laws remain, the more certain a person is of being able to carry out a program of action. Within such a democratic framework the people of the United States have had unusual opportunities to develop their personalities.

We say *have had* because the citizens of the United States have rapidly drifted away from the principles of democracy and toward fascism. In 1933 emergency laws passed by Congress gave the President greater powers than a president has ever had. He was given certain powers over money, and the right to change its value at any time. He was given power over Federal relief and other funds totaling billions of dollars. A number of other sweeping powers were bestowed on him.

We are not concerned here with political details except to point out that citizens, by their very votes, have been giving away their democracy and preparing themselves for fascism. Important farm laws, labor laws, laws for the control of business, have given new and sweeping powers to certain bureaus and boards. This process has limited and will increasingly limit the freedom of individuals to develop their personalities and their personal security.

The Supreme Court, already affected by the concept of liberalism, is in danger of becoming almost completely liberal. It may increasingly fail to declare void new laws which violate the Constitution. People, in their desire for the abundant life and social security, have more and more voted away their personal responsibilities and therefore their freedom and opportunities. To this extent they have abandoned democracy for fascism.

To that part of the population who never could manage themselves, this may be little loss. But to the great majority who would manage their own affairs, and whose abilities supported education and created employment, this is a serious loss. Their efforts are thrown into confusion, their initiative is stifled. The result has already been discord and increased unemployment which, with minor delays and possibly interrupting wars, will become increasingly disastrous.

COMMUNISM—THE NEGATION OF PERSONALITY

Communism, as described by Karl Marx, represents the almost complete denial of personality. The very term implies the opposite of individualism. Some people have compared communism with religion, mistaking passion for fervor. In religion, personality is the highest of all values. In communism personality is the lowest of all values. The religious martyr will die for a faith which has nothing to do with the goods of this world. The communist's faith has everything to do with the goods of this world. Because they are at opposite poles in theory, religion and communism are at war in practice. There is no room for either religious, intellectual, or political freedom under communism.

Communism is a purely economic scheme and its underlying objectives and methods are economic. Its very inception involves the seizure of property and goods by the proletariat. Its program is to divide material wealth as equally as possible among all good communists. It assumes that people are equal and must remain equal; at least through its attempts at equal distribution of wealth it has the effect of keeping down the able to the level of the unable. *The theory of communism is held more important than the communists themselves.* Although professing to give every individual an equal opportunity, it puts every individual in a strait-jacket instead. The state, not individuality, is supreme. Economic goods, not personality, are its goal.

This is communism in theory, and in much of its practice. Historically, communism in Russia may have done more for the people than did the dictatorship it overthrew. However, it has succeeded to the extent that it has given up the theories of Marx and recognized the values of personality and the psychology of individual differences. Its primary goal is still economic goods and physical wealth. This goal, standing alone, will not create but destroy personality.

A democracy like the United States can survive only through the personalities of its citizens. We may not be so far from communism as we think. The chief goal in our country has increasingly become economic wealth. The abundant life materially has become the end most quickly and passionately sought, and to such an extent that the gold standards of morals and religion have been increasingly sacrificed.

Justice Brandeis said, in 1923: "Democracy substitutes self-restraint for external restraint. It demands continuous sacrifice by the individual and more exigent obedience to the moral law than any other form of government." A democracy which does not put the religious and moral values of personality above the achievement of the abundant life will achieve neither. If, through the communistic principles of covetousness and socialized stealing, our democracy artificially distributes wealth, it will be found that poverty and slavery have been distributed instead. *For there can be no political distribution of character and personality. Only personalities can create wealth, but wealth cannot create personalities.*

XI

THE PHILOSOPHY OF PERSONALITY

XI

THE PHILOSOPHY OF
PERSONALITY

THERE is one philosophy, the very heart of which is personality, that is the philosophy represented by Christianity. The essence of Christianity is its insistence on the supreme value of the individual in a scheme of things where love, faith, and moral law transcend all man's intellectual schemes and mechanical concepts.

In Christianity men are not the puppets of the state; they are the sons of God. They are not cogs in a machine but creatures with souls. They are not helpless victims of an adverse environment but rather beings born in sin —that is, subject to human weakness—bound to suffer for their sins, but possessing the power to be born again to a new life of unlimited growth and freedom.

No matter how individuals, differing in background and point of view, read the New Testament, they will agree that its common denominator is the *potentiality of personality*. All men are held equal in the opportunity to develop a richer personality and a higher life, whether Jew or Gentile, Pharisee or publican, rich or poor, whole or crippled. If anything, the possibilities of the underprivileged excel those of the privileged. For the rich, salvation is more difficult than to enter through the eye of a needle; for the arrogant intellectual, it is harder than for the ignorant but repentant sinner. But for all it is possible.

Thus the Christian concept of personality is the absolute opposite to that of the physical sciences. Whereas the natural sciences have progressively revealed man's limitations, Christianity forever emphasizes his possibilities. Whereas the mental hygiene movement of medical science increasingly describes people as innocent victims of mental disorders, Christianity long ago described the same disorders as the natural consequences of sin—either the sins of omission or of commission. The doctrine of sin and salvation, so vital a part of Christianity, is but the declaration of faith in man's power to achieve personality, his errors notwithstanding.

Even the doctrine of immortality, so frowned on by science, becomes in Christianity a dramatic expression of the supreme value of personality. The soul, not the political or economic system, lives on. The individual, not the state, has ultimate value. Therefore the state exists for the individual, as in democracy, and not the individual for the state, as in fascism and communism. Indeed, the rise of Christianity as a power in western civilization rests squarely on the doctrine that citizenship in the immortal kingdom of God is far more important than life in any temporal kingdom. This very concept has made democracy as we know it possible, because Christianity has insisted on a minimum of regimentation by any temporal government so that the individual could assume a maximum personal responsibility in a permanent kingdom of spiritual values.

The tragedy of the Christian Church is that she has tried to make a compromise with science instead of consistently denying the power of science to touch the soul of man. The Church, or at least a large part of the Church, has surrendered many of the eternal truths of personality to the interpretations of science and the social studies. The sciences and even pseudo-sciences have to a large extent been allowed to usurp the authority of the Church and religion over personality and its development.

Thus science has been permitted to shift the emphasis from the doctrine of immortality, which looks forward, to the doctrine of heredity, which looks backward.

Instead of the conviction of sin and personal responsibility, we now have the reputable, if pseudo-scientific definition of the unconscious mind, which permits a person to commit sins without being considered responsible.

In place of the religious belief that man is born in sin, but can be born again to a better life and better habits, we now have the doctrine that he must get rid of his inhibitions.

The natural selfishness of man has been rationalized and even idealized through the social philosophy of self-expression and living one's own life.

The religious belief that man must suffer for his shortcomings either in a hell hereafter or a hell on earth has been condemned as being a negative gospel of fear. Now people are described as suffering from phobias and all manner of pseudo-scientific compulsions which have no place in the Church catechism, but which are filling the mental hospitals at an appalling rate.

The true physician of the soul and many of the current emotional disorders should be the ministry, yet large portions of the Church have delegated this basic duty to the machinists of the soul.

The need for a program of *mental hygiene* in all fields of education is now widely recognized. Mental hygiene refers primarily to the problems of personality here described. Yet mental hygiene in the United States is developing as primarily a medical program with the many fallacies which this approach represents. Mental hygiene should logically be the basic educational program of the Church, and even its secular contents should be inspired by religious truths.

Whatever happens to the Church in its present form, the basic truths of Christianity will survive so long as man and human nature survive; because these truths are the foundations of personality and character. If, as Thomas Mann has said, Democracy is inevitable, this is true only insofar as the acceptance of Christianity is inevitable. The rediscovery of man through the scientific experiments of psychology is a vindication of the Biblical concept of personality and of the precepts of Christianity. There is simply no escape from that great definition of personality: "For whosoever will save his life shall lose it: and whosoever will lose his life for my sake shall find it." Self-sacrifice and service are here the basis of personality, a concept quite consistent with our psychological definition: Personality is measured by the extent to which the individual has learned to convert his energies into habits and skills which interest and serve others. Jesus preached and lived the doctrine of service, even to the extent of washing his disciples' feet.

However, the Christian concept of personality does not stop with the precepts of service, of loving one's neighbor, of being one's brother's keeper. All these aspects of personality are predicated on the concept of obedience to the moral law. These laws, beginning with the Ten Commandments, represent the highest rules in the game of life, and God the highest of all umpires. Jesus extended the moral laws of the Old Testament and widened their application. Subsequently the Christian Church had an enormous influence on the codification of secular laws. The early history of the United States and the Constitution strongly reflect Christian doctrines.

In modern times, however, a large part of the Church has ceased to extend or to amplify the moral law. Quite the contrary, the academic doctrine of liberal interpretations has increasingly influenced the Church, some sections more than others. Paradoxically, the denominations have remained conservative and orthodox in respect to the theological and ritualistic minutiae which separate them and which may be no more important than the formalistic doctrines of the Pharisees were in the eyes of Christ; whereas in respect to the Commandments and the teachings of Jesus and Paul which are of vital importance, the Church has become so liberal as to lose much of her authority. An umpire who does not interpret the rules with growing definiteness and consistency naturally ceases to be an umpire.

For example, the religious morals of marriage, once so highly codified by the Church through the marriage ceremony, have been given more and more liberal interpretations. Many denominations have gradually accepted the secular practices of marriage and divorce, and these are based on the theories of pleasure rather than the religious concept of duty. Thus the Church, at least the Protestant Church, has lost her moral authority over marriage and the family. Marriage has now become a subject for academic courses in college. Success in marriage is more a matter of intelligence than morals, of clever devices than of unswerving ideals.

Similarly, under the impact of scientific and pseudo-scientific theories, the Church has liberalized or sanctioned the liberal interpretations of other moral laws. The law, Honor thy father and thy mother, etc., has been sacrificed to the liberal philosophies of self-expression and to certain fads of education. The educators now, rather than the Church, interpret this law, and with a liberalism which has produced utmost confusion among parents and children.

The harmful effects of gambling on personality have become more and more obvious; yet the attitude of a large part of the Church toward gambling remains undetermined and contradictory.

The Commandments, Thou shalt not covet, and Thou shalt not steal, were not extended by the Church to the condemnation of the profit motive in places where profits were at the expense of personality. It would probably have been better to have fewer and more expensive automobiles if, thereby, the enslavement of workers to a few repetitive motions could have been avoided. This is only one of many situations where profits might properly have been classified as a form of stealing or of covetousness. Having failed to develop the social implications of these Commandments in the past, it is not surprising that the new *socio-economic gospel* can now interpret socialized stealing as a virtue, and short-cuts to the distribution of wealth as social justice. The pattern of liberal interpretation, in the Church as in secular life, can justify almost any means in trying to achieve a modern kingdom of heaven.

This very tendency to interpret the morals of life more liberally instead of more definitely has undermined the power of the Church's appeals for a spiritual re-awakening. There have been many awakenings. Many people are today eager to accept a more spiritual interpretation of the universe and of personality. However, they cannot accept the moral ambiguities of the Church as the equivalent of spiritual values, nor her liberal uncertainties as the verities of religion. The yearning for spiritual truth is a revolt against the confusing multiplicities of liberal truths. It is a willingness to accept by faith and authority a way of life which puts goodness above goods, and the rules of the game above the achievement of victory or abundance.

Therefore the Church will have no authority until she speaks with authority, and she cannot speak with authority until she has again resumed her rôle of interpreting Christian morals with greater definiteness and less liberalism. "For he taught them as one having authority and not as the scribes."

Maybe it is too late for the Church to take this revolutionary step, involving as it does a right-about face and a march often directly against the present educational and social trends. Maybe only another great teacher and law-giver can succeed in bringing the moral law up to date. In the meanwhile, psychology reveals the vacuum now existing in the codes of personality, and the absolute need for the development of codes in this field. Furthermore, psychology has discovered the methods by which codes operate, as, for example, in competitive sports. The rules of the game are more important than the individual while playing, and sportsmanship is more important than victory. Indeed, the many detailed findings in respect to personality tend to prove that the old-fashioned Commandments are amazingly true to human nature as it now is, and should be interpreted far more literally and extensively than at present.

XII

THE SUPREME PERSONALITY

XII

THE SUPREME PERSONALITY

THE attempts of preachers on Easter Sundays to explain the resurrection of Jesus have often intrigued me. If we define personality as the power to interest and serve other people, is not Jesus the greatest living personality in the world today? To whom else do so many people pay active tribute on a Sunday or during the week? Who, daily, inspires the lives of so many people with faith in themselves and a desire to live up to his expectations?

In this country we celebrate the birthdays of Washington and Lincoln, but His birthday we celebrate through Christmas and all the activities of a Christmas season—and he not even a citizen! With much of the world we commemorate his crucifixion and his deathless personality through the Lenten season and the Easter holidays.

Truly no personality who now walks the earth begins to be alive compared with the living influence of Jesus!

Jesus was a great liberal but in a sense quite different from that represented by the popular current liberalism.

His liberalism was based on a reaffirmation of the ancient law. Even when most critical of the existing order and the formalism of the Pharisees, he defined his liberalism as follows: "Think not that I am come to destroy the law, or the prophets: I am not come to destroy but to fulfil. For verily I say unto you, Till heaven and earth pass, one jot or one tittle shall in no wise pass from the law, till all be fulfilled. Whosoever therefore shall break one of these least commandments, and shall teach men so, he shall be called the least in the kingdom of heaven."

Here, as elsewhere, he accepted the Ten Commandments as they stood. Instead of liberalizing them, he expanded them into a more definite and comprehensive application to the details of life. He rebuked the Pharisees for their devious logic in evading the commandment, Honor thy father and thy mother. The commandment, Thou shalt not commit adultery, he expanded so far as to include among other amendments, this: "Whosoever looketh on a woman to lust after her hath committed adultery with her already in his heart." The commandment, Thou shalt not covet, he interpreted in considerable detail and with special reference to both poor and rich.

When the rich young man asked Jesus what he must do to have eternal life, Jesus told him to keep the commandments. When he asked, which, Jesus named five of the Ten Commandments and this: "Thou shalt love thy neighbor as thyself." All these, the young man affirmed, he had kept from his youth up. Only then did Jesus say: "If thou wilt be perfect, go and sell that thou hast, and give to the poor, and thou shalt have treasure in heaven: and come and follow me."

Thus Jesus consistently tested the new by the old, rather than the old by the new. Even though he was instigating a radically new social order, it was one more firmly than ever based on the old moral law. He amplified the laws and the prophets much as the rules in competitive sports are developed—not by a process of repudiation or substitution, but by using the foundation already given. His liberalism was like that of the modern scientist: he began with axioms already demonstrated and built upon this foundation. It was the exact opposite of the modern liberalism among jurists who regard the interpretations of lawyers as more important than the law itself.

Jesus was an interpreter, a reformer. He believed that the law was made for man and not man for the law. However, he did not therefore believe that man, not even himself, could twist the law to suit his particular philosophy. To him the Ten Commandments were not the *folklore of capitalism* nor the folklore of any other *ism*. They were the basic axioms of personality under any economic system. They were the guideposts through any period of social reform. They were the very foundation for the brotherhood of man, the very bulwark against the barbaric theory that might makes right.

Jesus' subordination of his own reason and ambitions to the existing law is nowhere better demonstrated than in the stories of the temptation. After Jesus had fasted forty days, Satan tempted him to command that the stones around him be turned to bread. Jesus answered:

"It is written: Man shall not live by bread alone but by every word that proceedeth out of the mouth of God." Again Satan tempted him, and again the reply was: *It is written* . . . Finally Satan took him up on a high mountain and promised to give him all the great kingdoms he could see for the simple act of falling down and worshiping him. The reply was: "Get thee hence, Satan: for it is written, Thou shalt worship the Lord thy God, and Him only shalt thou serve."

The analogy between the story of the temptation and the history of our times is remarkable. Jesus was tempted by a vision of speedy power and popularity if he would but discard tradition for expediency. His answer was: "It is written." Instead of a few disciples trained by laborious teaching, he could have had a whole kingdom of lands and people merely by resorting to a few simple devices. His verdict was: "It is written." Instead of achieving a doubtful success in time, he could have achieved it at once by discarding his old-fashioned ideals for more practical methods. But again his answer was: "It is written."

Jesus is the great liberal of all time, yet his mission was one of fulfilling rather than repudiating the old order. He was a conservative first and a progressive afterward. Instead of deprecating the moral axioms of the Old Testament, he made them the foundation for his new structure. Though he built slowly, he built with a permanence and with a type of values which make him supreme among personalities even today.

His goal was the Kingdom of God, but not by short-cuts which would destroy personality in the process.

Indeed, his great contribution to man was a concept of personality far above any yet conceived. Personality was a force that transcended any form of earthly government, any system of economics, any ritualistic or intellectual order. But further, he formulated codes of action by which personality could be achieved, he gave authority to these codes, and he inspired man with the confidence that he could achieve his highest personality under these codes.

Other men have given their lives for their faith, or done great deeds for humanity; but this was Christ's great gift to man: a concept of freedom through the moral law. Christ is the great Liberator of man from his own follies. He is the prophet of the potential greatness in all men!

Psychology now confirms and elaborates, by the methods of modern science, what Christ proclaimed through prophetic insight, namely:

That sportsmanship is more important than winning the game.

That short-cuts to the abundant life destroy personality.

That the principle of expediency, namely, the end justifies the means, leads to mental and moral anarchy.

That playing the games of life according to the rules is more important than pre-occupation with the rules themselves.

That is to say, personality is the result of faith rather than of reason, of action more than of thought, of observing the laws rather than of interpreting them into new laws.

The faith of the individual in himself, in his fellow men, and in a higher moral order, we are discovering, is more important than all the knowledge which the natural sciences have given us.

Team-work, we find, is the very foundation of personal and social happiness; but team-work is impossible without codes and morals accepted by individuals voluntarily.

Personal, national, and international relationships are dependent on a moral code which applies equally to all, and without *preferred interpretations.*

Jesus went back into history for the basic moral law, the Commandments. Upon these he built his further codes for humanity, through a religious insight or an intuitive grasp of human nature.

These codes and morals have been lost sight of. They have been obscured by the multiplicities of science and education. In cracking the secrets of the atom, we have lost the secrets of man.

Now psychology discovers or rediscovers the axioms of living through the study of man himself. The Ten Commandments are not the mores or customs peculiar to a time and race; they are the basic and unchanging laws of personality! They are as axiomatic to social harmony as are the axioms of mathematics to the development of knowledge. Human nature can no more tolerate a liberal interpretation of its moral axioms than science can of its mathematical axioms.

The times and the circumstances may change, but the axioms of human nature do not change, any more than do the axioms of science. The streamlined personality or society today is not basically different from that two thousand years ago.

The great task before us, therefore, is first, to discover and to establish the axioms of personality. Second, to extend and to codify these axioms in terms of the personal and social concepts of living. This book represents a step in that direction.

Whether the science of psychology can accomplish this task in time to avert the impending crash of our present civilization is open to question. Whether the Church and its present leaders will appreciate this problem and act on it in time is also doubtful. Maybe the times are ripe for the appearance of another great prophet, like Jesus, who can give the world a moral code through intuition and revelation. Maybe nothing but universal disaster and suffering will prepare people for an appreciation of the fundamentals of life.

In the meanwhile, every individual must decide for himself whether he will drift with the stream or try to swim up-stream, that is, be an idealist rather than a realist, a person of definite principles rather than an opportunist, a conservative whose loyalties can be counted on rather than a liberal whose chief loyalty is the conviction that he can change his mind.

APPENDIX

APPENDIX

Bibliography

GREAT EXPERIMENTS IN PSYCHOLOGY, H. E. Garrett, New York, Appleton-Century, 1930. Usually when people ask me for a book which will give them an idea of the real nature of psychology, and if I think that the person making the request may become seriously interested in psychology as a science, I recommend this book. It describes in language which is properly technical but not too technical some of the outstanding experimental discoveries in psychology such as: the studies leading to the development of the I.Q.; Watson's studies of behavior of infants; Cattell's experiments in measuring reaction time; Galton's measurement of individual differences; etc. The one important gap in this book is its failure to deal with the great experiments in the field of personality made especially during the past fifteen years.

PRINCIPLES OF PSYCHOLOGY, William James, New York, Holt, 1908. For a person who wishes to read a book on psychology with applications to himself and his own improvement, James' book is, in my opinion, still one of the best, if not the best. It deals with such subjects as habits and their formation, will-power, the emotions, memory, etc. Moreover, it discusses these problems in a fascinating and readable style. Although over thirty years old, the psychology of James is more up-to-date today than it was at the time of its writing. That is to say, the importance of the principles and facts emphasized by James have been increasingly demonstrated as being the really important phases of psychology. For example, the basic importance of habit in the total psychological picture is better recognized today than it was thirty years ago.

THE RETURN TO RELIGION, Henry C. Link, Macmillan, New York, 1936. Quite a few people have deplored to me the title of this book. "If you had not used the term *religion* many more people would have read it," is their usual remark. "After all it is quite unlike anything a person expects under the name, religion," they also say. There is much in what these friendly critics have claimed. Nevertheless, I have never really regretted the title. One clergyman remarked: "As a book on religion it is really a good book on psychology." He saw the point, namely, that psychology was proving, through its studies, that religion was the very foundation of personality. The title might have been: Psychology and Religion. In spite of its title, nearly one hundred and fifty thousand people have bought the book and many more have read it. What has given me the greatest satisfaction is the practical use made of the book by children and young people from sixteen years through college.

THE POLICIES AND PRACTICES OF THE PSYCHO-LOGICAL SERVICE CENTER, an article in the August, 1938 issue of the *Journal of Consulting Psychology* prepared by Henry C. Link with the assistance of his associates, Drs. P. S. Achilles, Rose G. Anderson, R. S. Schultz, G. K. Bennett.

THE PSYCHOLOGY OF FUNCTIONAL NEUROSES, H. L. Hollingworth, New York, Appleton, 1920. This is a statement of the Freudian doctrines of psychoanalysis, and a criticism of these doctrines, by one of the leading psychologists. The Freudian theory of dreams, the unconscious mind, the libido, rationalization, projection, sublimation, etc., are described and evaluated.

MANUAL OF PSYCHIATRY, A. J. Rosanoff, New York, Wiley, 1927 (6th ed.). This is one of the best examples of the classical psychiatric treatment of abnormal behavior and is a standard work in this field.

A TEXT-BOOK OF PSYCHIATRY, D. K. Henderson and R. D. Gillespie, London, Oxford, 1932 (3rd ed.). This is a classic textbook on psychiatry in England, one covering the legitimate field of psychiatry as developed along traditional and yet progressive lines.

A BIOLOGICAL APPROACH TO THE PROBLEM OF ABNORMAL BEHAVIOR, Milton Harrington, M.D., Lancaster: Science Press, 1938. This is the latest and one of the very few books written by a psychiatrist which departs radically from the classical psychiatric treatment of abnormal behavior, and adopts the fundamental concepts of psychology and the principles of habit formation in describing human behavior. It also leans heavily on physiology and physiological psychology. This is a highly technical and professional book, and is mentioned here principally as one important evidence of the trend just getting under way in the psychiatric field, a trend which has thus far made very little headway. Dr. Harrington is also the author of an "analysis of psychoanalysis" in which he sets forth his reasons for rejecting psychoanalysis.

JOURNAL OF APPLIED PSYCHOLOGY, James P. Porter, Editor, Ohio University, Athens, Ohio; Paul S. Achilles and Henry C. Link, co-editors. This Journal which is published every two months is one of the many journals in the field of psychology. However, it is unique in that it is the only authoritative journal to devote itself entirely to the practical applications of scientific psychology. For twenty-one years it has been the recognized vehicle for the publication of experiments which have practical results. It may be read by laymen who are interested in the developments in the field of applied psychology.